Contents

Touching Tomorrow

The Story of Hephzibah Children's Home

Sandy Neal

by Alberta Metz

Updated by Dr. Ronald R. Brannon

Dedication

This book is dedicated to all the past and present staff
members whose sacrificial service has made
Hephzibah Children's Home possible since 1900.

Forward

Touching Tomorrow: The Story of Hephzibah Children's Home and what a story it is! It tells it just as it is . . . the sublime and the ridiculous; the sad and humorous; the favorable and unfavorable; the expectations and disappointments.

Hephzibah Alumni have "touched tomorrow" in remarkable ways—preachers, missionaries, teachers, doctors, ministers' wives, business leaders, soldiers, and committed lay persons. In many cases this would not have happened had there been no Hephzibah. Her alumni are from orphaned families, broken homes, and wards of the court. Yet their contributions to society are significant and, in some instances, exceed those who do not have these obstacles to overcome.

Hephzibah Children's Home is the tangible expression of the social conscience of The Wesleyan Church pertaining to this phase of its Christian obligation. It is a positive affirmation that she is caring, compassionate and concerned for the less fortunate. The leadership and financial support given since 1922 has been constant and continues today on an increasing scale. It must be accelerated.

Alberta R. Metz has graphically portrayed the Hephzibah story. The early pioneers were without earthly prospects. But with the eye of faith they caught Elishu's vision of horses and chariots and a host of friends coming to their rescue. Events have been encountered when food and essential items had to literally "be prayed in," reminiscent of those faced by George Mueller, the great man of faith, who operated several orphanages in England. What a tonic to our faith in this materialistic age.

God has supplied the needs in mysterious ways. A truck loaded with chickens broke down in front of the Home. The driver requested the use of the telephone to call his buyers in Atlanta. They suggested he sell them in Macon. He tried but failed. He gave them to the Home. Georgia "revenuers" captured canning jars and bags of sugar from a moonshiner's still and decided to give them to Hephzibah—just in time for the canning season. One of the workers had a tax obligation of $18.00 without money to pay it. She found a twenty dollar bill fluttering in the breeze near the street curb. She decided it was similar to Peter who found his tax money in a fish's mouth. Many other needs were supplied in fascinating ways.

Dedication has been the trademark of the leaders and staff from Bettie Tyler in 1900 until Larry Freels of the present. Typical of many, it was said of one: "She traveled for the Home until her feet gave out, and then she wrote those who contributed until her hands gave out." Dedication must become the trademark of all wherever situated, not merely by the Hephzibah staff.

This second edition recounts what God has done at Hephzibah Children's Home during the 90s. Dr. Ronald R. Brannon, General Secretary of The Wesleyan Church, was asked to help do the updating because of his involvement with Hephzibah as a member of the Board of Directors. He has been one of the prime movers in the progress made and is aware of the importance of preserving the significant events in Hephzibah's history. He has shown that through the Lord, the impossible became possible again and again.

This challenging story must be read and retold again and again. "Hephzibah" means "my delight is in her." The contents of this book will convince you that God's delight is in the "Hephzibah" mentioned in Isaiah 62:4 and also in the "Hephzibah" located in Macon, Georgia.

Virgil A. Mitchell
Former Chairman of the Hephzibah Board
General Superintendent Emeritus

Preface

Nations, institutions, families and individuals often sense a need to create a written record of the past—to inform, to teach, to explain and to enjoy. This history of Hephzibah Children's Home in Macon, Georgia, has been written for all those reasons. But histories tend to be rather dull and dry. Webster's first definition for the word "history" is "tale, story." Any history is exciting, not because of those indispensable dates and prosaic facts, but because of the "tales and stories" that enliven the dusty annals. So our purpose has been not only to uncover dates and facts, but to discover all the intriguing episodes treasured in people's memories. Perhaps some will be disappointed to find certain names left out. Scores of staff members and hundreds of children are part of the Hephzibah story. It is impossible to mention them all. Those whose stories are told are representative of the rest.

Director Joe Neyman remarked, "If we're going to get a history written, now is the time, for in a few years many of the people will be gone." On a trip to Hephzibah in September 1988, I was able to tape interviews with Grace Tyler Palmer, age 91, niece of Hephzibah's founder, Bettie Tyler; Mrs. D. L. Jones, widow of the superintendent from 1931 to 1942; Annie Pearl Crawford Welsh, a resident of the Home in the early days; Mrs. Dorothy Allison, housemother from 1955 to 1979; as well as many current staff members and some former residents.

Resources in the Washington Memorial Library in Macon shed light on the early days and provided copies of the newspaper articles covering the 1912 fires. Previous histories of the Home gave 1910 as the date for that event.

Telephone calls, letters, cassette tapes and *Hephzibah Happenings* (newsletter) have furnished much material. A college course paper on Hephzibah by Rodney Weaver was helpful.

This story is "fictionalized" only in the actual words said, for example, by Bettie and Mollie Tyler. No events have been fabricated. Not all the stories from all the interviews synchronized perfectly. Many discrepancies surfaced, and this is not surprising when people try to recall events of the distant past. Annie Pearl Crawford Welsh had a pamphlet written by Bettie Tyler telling something of the founding of the orphanage. Incidentally, the letter from Bettie to J. H. Lawrence was signed by Bettie, thus providing the spelling of her name.

Joe and Shirley Neyman squeezed time from their hectic schedule to talk with me. (However, Shirley told me more about Joe than he did!) Mike Manley, director of development at Hephzibah, served as "liaison," tracking down details, answering questions, doing interviews, and getting copies made of photos. His valuable help is acknowledged and appreciated. He and his wife were my hosts during my visit to Macon and furnished needed transportation.

Dan Burnett, archivist at The International Center—The Wesleyan Church, was helpful in providing resources. My sister, Alice Wills, librarian at Indiana Wesleyan University, Marion, Indiana, gave much-needed guidance in computerizing and printing out the manuscript. My daughter, Lydia Hines, was the first one to read the manuscript and she offered valuable suggestions. My mother, Ruth Bowman, and my husband, Rev. Floyd Metz, were my support team who prayed faithfully for me during the weeks I worked on the project.

Friends at my local church, Marion Brookhaven, were also supportive. Three men taught my adult Sunday school class for several Sundays so I could spend more time on the book.

Highest praise goes to my Heavenly Father to whom I turned daily for wisdom and guidance. My prayer is that He will use this book to glorify himself, to bring readers closer to Him and to inspire prayer and giving for a wonderful institution that continues to touch tomorrow.

Alberta Metz
1989

Acknowledgements

Many thanks to Shirley Duncan and Dr. Ronald Brannon for their work in updating the story of Hephzibah Children's Home.

Chapter I

Looking For Love

Shirley Ann trembled as she crouched under the porch, fear knotting her stomach. Sounds of fighting and yelling were coming from the tiny three-bedroom house across the road. When her mother and step-father started fighting, she always ran out of their house to one of her "hidey-holes." Putting her fingers in her ears she cried and waited until the fight was over and her mother would come looking for her.

The tall, thin, red-eyed man who had married her mother was mean when he was drunk. "I hate him!" Shirley whispered. "I hate this kind of life!"

Her longing for a better way of living had grown as she attended church with Grandpa and Grandma Locklear. She knew there was a better way to live. Grandpa and Grandma loved her, cared for her whenever they could, and helped make life bearable. Their house was nearby on one of the dirt roads that tied their little community together. The Locklears were members of the Lumbee Indian tribe, which lived in Robeson County, North Carolina, and there were many of them in this section of the town of Lumberton.

When Shirley was five years old, (she was born in 1958), Grandma became quite ill. Shirley went to see her and found her, thin and frail, lying in bed. Grandpa stood at the foot of the bed while she talked to her grandmother. They called their granddaughter Shirlann, like everyone else did. It was a long time before she knew her name was Shirley Ann.

"I love you," Grandma said to her. "Keep your pretty hair combed every day. John, take good care of Shirlann and buy her lots of pretty dresses."

Grandpa nodded slowly and sadly.

Shirley never forgot what her grandmother told her before she died.

One rainy day Shirley's step-father said to her, "Get yourself over yonder and get me some liquor!"

*Shirley Ann Locklear
as a child*

"Yes, Sir." Shirley's heart sank, but she dared not raise any objections. Leaving the house, she walked along the dirt road past little country stores and small houses. After a time she left the road, jumped over a little creek and began walking across a plowed field. She had been this way many times.

What if wolves come and get me? she thought, fear making her hurry, the cold mud pressing into her torn, broken shoes. Another ditch to jump over, another field to cross and at last she was knocking at the door of a house. The Indian woman took the money and gave her a small bottle in a paper sack. How could Shirley know the woman was a bootlegger and selling the liquor illegally?

Back across the fields she went, shivering from cold and from fear. In her hands she was carrying the very thing that turned their little house into a hell on earth.

Shirley and her half-brother and half-sister did their best to stay out of their father's way. One wrong move and they could be in for a beating. That went for their mother too. One day Shirley became the object of his wrath and he beat her savagely.

"Stop it! Stop it! Leave her alone!" screamed her mother.

In his rage he turned on his wife, kicking her and cursing.

Shirley, sobbing in terror and pain, looked down to see blood running down her legs from the wounds he had inflicted. Was there no place of safety, no place where she could find love?

One day her mother was mixing up dough for biscuits and had put the flour in a large aluminum pan. Shirley was sitting on the couch (which was also her bed) watching TV. Her little sister was sitting on the kitchen floor under the table.

Suddenly everyone got deathly still, for the man of the house had walked in. His family looked at him to see what his mood was.

"What're you lookin' at?" he yelled at his wife. Grabbing up the pan of flour he dumped it on her head. She screamed and cried and he began beating her.

By this time Shirley was out the front door. But suddenly something stopped her and she ran back into the house. Her step-father had gone into the bedroom and came out with a shotgun. Terrified, Shirley grabbed her little sister from the floor and ran outside. A gunshot pierced the air. Had he shot their mother?

Later Shirley returned to find everyone safe. But to her horror she saw a bullet hole right where her little sister had been.

When her step-father was not there, Shirley often begged her mother to leave their home in Lumberton. "Let's move, Mother. Let's leave here. Let's go to High Point to Aunt Verdie's!"

Shirley's mother was uneducated and hardly able to read. Perhaps her only security was in the tiny three-room house with her husband. But one day she was so angry and afraid she got the three children into the car and drove madly down the dirt road.

"I'll kill us before he does!" she cried.

"Mama!" Shirley screamed. "Mama! Let me out of here! Don't do this!"

Finally the distraught woman slowed the car down and let Shirley out. The frightened girl walked home.

One December Shirley's step-father would not let her mother use any money to buy her anything for Christmas. On Christmas morning her brother and sister opened presents while she sat and watched.

Hatred intensified in her heart. She hated her mother, too, for letting this man dictate to her and run their lives.

Grandpa Locklear, fearing for the family's safety, urged them to leave Lumberton. Finally the mother decided to take his advice. A new chapter opened in Shirley's life.

After they were settled in High Point, Shirley got acquainted with Mr. and Mrs. Asbury who lived across the street. Helen Asbury invited her to go to church with them. Thus began a love affair with the Hayworth Wesleyan Church. Those people became her people. The older ladies were her grandmothers. Her Sunday school teacher was like a mother. She felt loved. Helen took her to church on Wednesday nights and they stopped at Mayberry's for ice cream afterward.

It was wonderful to be away from her step-father, but life at home was not happy for Shirley. Being the oldest child and large for her age, she was left to baby-sit and was expected to clean house and pay bills— or else lie to the creditors to keep from paying. Shirley hated it.

Then her mother began dating another man. This made the girl hate her mother all the more. She didn't trust or like men at all. Why would her mother want to get involved with someone and have all that trouble start again?

She found every way she could to stay away from home. Her mother and sister and brother thought she was "uppity," that she put herself above them.

One day Shirley got sick at school. Her stomach hurt and her side ached. When she got home her mother was getting ready to leave for work. "Take some aspirin and go to bed," her mother told her.

But that's not what Shirley wanted to do. She had to convince someone she was really sick. In the bathroom she painted Merthiolate on her cheeks so she would look feverish. Then she walked down the street two blocks to an upstairs apartment where two ladies from the church lived. Unable to convince them of her need for medical help, she decided she would go to the emergency room of the hospital. If nothing else, her experience with life had taught her to be independent!

Walking down the street another few blocks, she went into the hospital emergency room. The first thing they wanted to know was where her mother was. Shirley didn't really want her mother in on this. "I don't have a mother. She's dead."

"Where's your guardian?"

"I don't have one of them either. But I'm sick. My stomach hurts and my side hurts."

Sally Edmonds, one of her friends from the church, worked in the hospital and she eventually identified this stubborn little stranger. In the midst of all this, the doctors discovered Shirley had appendicitis. Her mother was called in to sign the papers for surgery.

When the time came for her to be dismissed from the hospital, Shirley absolutely refused to go back home. Social service workers stepped in and Shirley was released into the care of Pauline and Sally Edmonds, members at Hayworth. Two weeks later she was placed with foster parents who were also members at Hayworth. She was the sixth foster child they had. This was a temporary placement.

The next foster home was not with Christian people. The Browns* had two boys of their own and a foster child, a boy named Johnny. To Shirley's disgust she had to share a bedroom with the three little boys! When the social worker came to visit, Mrs. Brown showed her a room across the hall and said that was where Shirley slept.

The Browns were on the go a lot and now they had a live-in baby-sitter. Their friends even brought their children and left them for Shirley to keep. The only bright spot in Shirley's life was the Hayworth church. She poured out her heart to her friends on the telephone.

Where could she turn? She had given her heart to the Lord. Could He give her the refuge she needed?

The story of the refuge she finally found began with an amazing lady who was born almost one hundred years before Shirley was.

*Not real name

The Vine Is Planted

he Civil War stretched long, cruel fingers into Georgia's cities, hamlets and farmhouses. They reached into the rural community of Bolingbroke in Monroe County a few miles from Macon.

Out on Pea Ridge Road, Sarah Tyler raised her brood of four—Sarah Elizabeth, Mary Ann, George and Willis. Every Sunday Sarah took her children to the Old Salem Methodist Church, which her husband's parents had helped found back in 1826. There the congregation prayed for the safe return of their soldiers, Sarah's husband among them. But Sarah took her children to church by herself for many years, for Thomas Tyler did not come back.

The Tyler children were converted and grew up to serve the Lord. Bettie (Sarah Elizabeth), an intelligent, persevering child, decided she would be a teacher. In the town of Forsyth she attended a school called Forsyth Female Collegiate Institute, now known as Tift College. A good student, she became an outstanding teacher, known in middle Georgia. Prim and proper, Bettie was devoted to her church and to her family, supporting her mother until Mrs. Tyler passed away.

Then a circuit-riding revivalist came to Old Salem Church. Rev. W. A. Dodge lived in Atlanta and took the train to his charge, where he kept a horse and buggy. Traveling the circuit he preached holiness and held wonderful revivals. Old Salem Church was

17

transformed. The Tyler young people were genuinely sanctified, along with many others.

Bettie laid her education, her refinement, and her formal but fruitless religion on the altar and experienced a recharging of divine energy. The prim schoolteacher became a power-filled soul-winner, testifying at every opportunity.

News reached the Tylers of a live-wire Free Methodist preacher who had begun a mission work in Atlanta. His name was E. E. Shelhamer. This fired-up Yankee managed to get his name in the southern papers rather often. Bettie and Mollie (Mary Ann) decided to cast their lot with him for awhile.

They joined a growing group of home and foreign missionaries who came to Shelhamer's Missionary Training Home. In amazing ways God prospered the work of the mission and the training home, miraculously providing for needs and generally confounding the opposition. The Tylers saw God in action!

But the leader and the work received a crushing blow when Mrs. Shelhamer (his first wife) died. Bettie and Mollie went to Macon and were soon involved in mission work there, first on Hazel Street and then in a warehouse near the union depot.

But Bettie's calling was not to be in city mission work. One of Bettie's aunts died, leaving her husband, Mr. Thompson, with four little boys, ages two to eight.

How is that poor man going to take care of those children? everyone wondered. He soon found out that he couldn't, and he tried to find someone to take them in. Perhaps he thought that since Bettie and Mollie were in mission work they could extend their concern to four little boys.

One day the four Thompson boys were left in Bettie's care. There they stood in stairsteps—Clarence, Ollie, Frank and Arnold.

Something turned over in Bettie's heart. She knew she had reached a milestone in her work for the Lord.

Bettie and Mollie made the children comfortable. Then the sisters went to prayer.

"God is calling me to undertake a work with orphans," Bettie told Mollie later.

"We can't keep children here," Mollie said.

"No, but God will provide a place. We must get what resources we have together."

As they made their preparations, they were reminded of the old farmhouse where they had been born and raised. The 600-acre property had been left to the four Tyler children.

"I'm sure the house isn't in very good shape," said Mollie.

Hephzibah's first home in Bolingbroke, Georgia, 1900

"But it will be our own place," replied Bettie. "Now what do we have on hand?"

That proved to be pitifully small: fifty cents' worth of sugar, a few pounds of rice, one dollar in cash—plus four little boys, two spinsters, and a God-given stock of faith and courage.

Not many of their friends looked on this plan with favor.

"It's a wild undertaking!" someone said. "Here it is the dead of winter and you not well, Bettie. You'll all freeze or starve!"

From the human view it did appear foolhardy. The little group of pioneers arrived at the dilapidated farmhouse in January of 1900. The older boys helped bring in wood for the old cookstove. Water had to be carried several hundred yards from the foot of the hill.

In Bettie's words, "We were without earthly prospects. But with an eye of faith we caught Elisha's vision of horses and chariots and a host of friends coming to our rescue."

Soon Mrs. Lillie Condon, a widow, came from New York with her four children. Needing a home for her family, she helped as a matron in the little orphanage.

One day in Atlanta, Mollie was walking along Capital Avenue when she heard a baby crying. Looking for the source of the cry, she discovered the infant on a doorstep of a vacant house. The police were called, investigation was made, the child was unclaimed, and it was taken to the orphanage. Gradually other children were added, among them a black boy named Sam who was adopted by the Tylers.

Bettie's sister and brothers sold their part of the farm to her, and she then had 600 acres, largely timber. She had a saw mill set up and workers began to saw logs into lumber. Expansion of the orphanage was imperative.

Willis Tyler, Bettie's brother, and his wife, Chattie, had their growing family on the farm, too. Everyone worked to raise vegetables,

Grace Tyler Palmer

milk cows, and provide for the increasing orphanage family. Houses were being built on the farm for the workers.

One day in 1904 the children and workers were sitting outside shelling peas. Chattie Tyler looked up and saw a funnel cloud coming toward them. "Come quick, children, come quick!" She herded them into the house. With a roar the tornado was upon them, but the house stood firm. When they ran outside they found that the partially built houses had been blown down.

As the months passed, Bettie felt the anguish of the lean times when faith was tested. Hearing the children cry for food and seeing the workers weak with hunger, she was driven to her knees, humbling herself before God with heartsearching and earnest prayers. Then help would come in a way that proved unmistakably that God had heard and answered.

At Hephzibah's homecoming in 1980, the visitors, former residents and their families, trekked out to the old Bolingbroke farm. Among them was John Harden, who had been brought to the orphanage in those early days at the age of six weeks. His mother was one of the matrons.

The *Macon Telegraph* published an account of the 1980 visit to the old farmhouse:

"Standing amid gray, peeling walls, near a rotting attic stairway in the old house, Harden patted a wooden doorjamb.

'That corner is where I slept,' he told a curious audience."

Grace (Palmer) and Mary (Battle), daughters of Willis Tyler, were also among the visitors. They remembered Bettie and Mollie, their aunts, tending a garden near the house, cooking meals and teaching Sunday school.

Efforts to enlarge their borders on the farm came to naught. Bettie sensed that the pillar of cloud was moving and they were to follow it to Macon. The year was 1906.

Chapter 3

Transplanted to Macon

Bettie stood gazing at the lovely house in amazement. This was to be the new home of her growing family. "My delight is in her." That was the meaning of Hephzibah, the Old Testament name she had decided to call the orphanage. Here in Vineville, just outside of Macon, God had led her to this beautiful place near Crump's Park.

Back on the farm, she told the children, "God has given us a new home with plenty of room." No more crowding pallets together on the attic floor, she thought.

But she didn't tell the children that she had no money for the first month's rent. Her meeting with the real estate agent was fresh in her mind.

"Yes, the house is exactly what we need," Bettie told him.

"And what backing do you have for this orphanage—a sponsor? a church?" His face was serious.

Bettie smiled. "No—none of those things. God is my only resource. He has not failed me before, and He will not fail me now."

The man searched her face as if to discover some evidence of derangement. "Humph! That won't do in my business! First month's rent must be paid in advance, Miss Tyler!"

Bettie smiled, nodded and left. She was confident God would not fail her. And, of course, He didn't! The Hephzibah family moved to its new home and the number of children and workers increased accordingly.

One year after the move Bettie was praying for needed rent money to come in. God's voice spoke plainly. "I want you to buy this place and I will pay for it if you will trust Me."

She knew what the selling price was. "Lord, we'll trust Thee for the $6000 required."

To her amazement she heard the Lord whisper, "Later I'll give you the building next door." He was as good as His word. Bettie was able to sell the Bolingbroke property and in a few years the orphanage complex covered half the block, and 75 children were being cared for. Babies had their own house, boys were in another, and girls were on the second floor of the staff house. The orphanage had its own school. As many as 100 children or more lived at one time at the Home at Crump's Park.

The children at Crump's Park enjoy a watermelon feast

Willis Tyler had become a Free Methodist minister. (Bettie and Mollie had also joined this denomination.) He and his family lived on the old farm for awhile after the orphanage moved to Macon. He brought produce, especially watermelons, to delight the children at Hephzibah. Sometimes the orphanage boys went out to help on the farm. Uncle Willis paid them a little money to hoe and weed. Later Willis moved his family to Macon.

Bettie decided the orphanage needed a broader administrative base. She arranged for a nondenominational board to be chosen. According to the minutes preserved from the 1910 meeting, Rev. T. W. Callaway became president of the board. Associate pastor of the Macon First Baptist Church, Rev. Callaway had a heart for the unreached lower class. Taking 22 members from First church, he started the Baptist Tabernacle.

Before long the Hephzibah children were attending. The church sent out a "band-wagon" to pick up the orphans, who must have been a

Bettie Tyler and her horse at the Crump's Park Home

lively addition to the tabernacle. Grace Tyler Palmer reports that the children got off the wagon yelling

Rah! Rah! Rah!
Sis boom bah!
Hephzibah Orphanage!
Ha! Ha! Ha!

A lover of children, Rev. Callaway haunted the probate court, petitioned for guardianship of orphans, and then brought them to Hephzibah.

During the years at Crump's park a lady came to Hephzibah who would have a far-reaching influence on the Home for over 50 years. Mrs. Lucile Ernest arrived, bringing her children, and worked first as a teacher in the orphanage. Later she became a solicitor, receiving a percentage of the money she raised. Willis Tyler also solicited for the Home.

Once again the work grew to such dimensions that more space was needed. Bettie was confident that God had a plan, but what was it?

ORPHANS HOMELESS THROUGH FLAMES

The headline made the front page of *The Macon Daily Telegraph* on Wednesday morning, June 19, 1912.

Early Tuesday evening a small fire was discovered under the main building. Investigation revealed a burning broom wedged between the timbers and the floor underneath the house. It was quickly put out. The children and staff gathered in the auditorium to give thanks to God for sparing them. But in the midst of their prayers the cry of "Fire!" was heard again. The back of the house was ablaze. Panic-stricken, the children began to scatter.

23

"Let's get our clothes! Hurry!" they cried.

"No, no! We will get your clothes!" The matrons quickly formed the children into lines and marched them to the other two cottages.

The now raging fire illuminated the night sky for two hours, bringing a large crowd to watch. The fire engines eventually arrived at the orphanage, which was outside the city limits. It was impossible to reach the building with water, and the two "chemical wagons" could not cope with the flames.

With concerted effort most of the clothing and bedding were saved, along with much of the furniture. These things were stored on the second floor of one of the other buildings.

Many homes—more than were needed—were offered to accommodate the children. The harried staff had all they could do to get everyone settled for the night.

Numbly Bettie tried to comprehend the extent of the loss. Gone was the beautiful three-room school building with the lovely new desks. Gone was the beautiful nine-room home, only twenty years old. Gone was the brick smokehouse in which a large order of supplies had been stored that very morning. The insurance could not possibly cover the loss.

How could it have happened? One of the matrons reported that a bathtub had overflowed for several hours that afternoon. She had noticed a light in the room below flickering off and on. Could the wiring have been affected by the water and caused the fire?

The Macon Daily Telegraph reported the blaze was of undetermined origin. Stories have filtered down through the years. Some believe that one of the girls who was upset over not getting her way, set the fire to get revenge. Another story suggests that a mischievous boy set a cat on fire and let it loose in the house. What actually happened will remain one of history's secrets.

Aunt Bettie was looking for a buyer for the orphanage. On Saturday, July 1, a real estate agent and a prospective buyer were to come and look at the damaged orphanage complex. That day the 30 children still left at the orphanage were eating their noon meal in one of the two small houses remaining. One of the older girls was sitting on the porch of the other house and became aware of heat coming from the wall. When she opened the door and flames leaped out, she ran to the other cottage to carry the news.

Terror once again gripped children and staff. Long agonizing minutes passed until the firemen, occupied with another fire, got permission from the mayor to dispatch part of their force to Vineville. But it was too late. The building where the salvaged articles from the first fire had been stored, now lay in ashes.

"Job's comforters" gathered around Bettie and her staff. "This is the end of Hephzibah," they said. "You can't expect people to come to your aid again. You could never have as nice a place as you had. God must be telling you to give up this work."

Bettie and her workers called mightily on God and one day the promise came in the words of Haggai. "The silver is mine and the gold is mine, saith the Lord of hosts." But, oh, the joy when her eyes fell on the next verse! "The glory of this latter house shall be greater than of the former, saith the Lord of hosts" (Haggai 2:8-9).

"God is going to give us a better place than we lost," Bettie told the workers. "He's got the silver and gold to do it!"

They sang together,

> *The baffled surf ebbs to the sea*
> *As though its task forsaking,*
> *But to return more mightily*
> *In greater volumes breaking.*

The very next day after God gave His promise, a lady they knew in California telegraphed $2000 to them.

Chapter 4

The Farm on Forsyth Road

Aunt Bettie found her "Promised Land" northwest of Macon on the highest point in Bibb County. Called "the Jacques place" or "the old West place," it was on the National Highway (later called Forsyth Road) that ran from New York to Jacksonville.

A beautiful, commodious two-story house stood on the hill overlooking a pecan orchard near the highway. Bettie and the orphanage board could see delightful prospects for this 67-acre farm with its fertile soil, pastures and woodlands.

The Vineville property was sold to Mr. Charles Cone for $7500. The new Hephzibah Orphanage would cost $25,000, and additional buildings would need to be erected at once. The Lord provided $21,000 to pay on the property and $9000 for improvements. The deed was signed on August 7, 1912.

The first building to be built was the dining hall/kitchen a hundred feet or so from the large house. Many friends from Macon came to help in the construction. Built on the side of a slope, the dining hall was on ground level with one side against the hill. A floor above that, on ground level at the top of the slope, was the boys' dormitory, one large room with a partition down the center, beds ranged in rows around the walls.

The main building, about 500 feet from the highway, was approached by a curving drive. A pillared porch ran around three sides

Children with workers in background, summer of 1919

Back Row: Bettie Tyler, Sarah Crawford, Wilma Riggs, Clara Yarbrough, Inez Josephson, Willie Wilson, Annie Pearl Crawford, Lucile Ernest.

Second Row: Gladys Millirons, Annie Mae Lingo, Ruby Braswell, Callie Temples, Bessie Burgess, Sallie Mae Dismuke.

Front Row: Annie Brannen, Helen McKinley, Mae Brannen, Doris Josephson (around 1921).

Bettie Tyler, founder

of the house. On the first floor was the dormitory for the little girls, rooms for workers and guests, a parlor, and a library. The older girls had a large dormitory on the second floor.

It was a happy day when the scattered Hephzibah family moved into their new home.

In those days getting from downtown Macon to the Home involved a 30-35 minute trolley ride (costing five cents) and then a long trek on a red clay road—either muddy or dusty—on foot or with a horse and wagon.

The people of Macon often sent boxes and baskets of food and clothing to the Home. One day Bettie was notified that a package was being delivered, but she would need to send someone to the road to pick it up. Two boys were assigned the task. When they got to the highway, there was a basket. Carrying it between them, they started back up the hill. Suddenly they heard a noise.

"What was that?"

"It—it came from the basket!"

"I'm scared! What d'you think it is?"

They stared at the bundle in the basket. Did something move?

"Let's hurry and take it to Aunt Bettie!"

When she received the strange gift, she pulled back the covering. There lay a tiny baby girl dressed in beautiful clothes. Bettie named the girl Elizabeth and she grew up at the Home.

Many times the Home was short on food and supplies. Once they ate their supper and knew there was nothing for breakfast. They began to pray. About three o'clock God woke up a grocer in Macon and told him about the need out on Forsyth Road. Just before breakfast time a two-horse wagon drove up to the orphanage with a load of groceries—no charge.

The boys did the farm chores and the girls, the household tasks. The city of Macon gave a hand pump to the Home for the well back of the dining hall. Near the well was a big black kettle. A fire was built under it and the clothes were boiled on laundry days. The boys kept the fire supplied with wood while the girls did the laundry.

Grace Tyler Palmer, Bettie Tyler's niece, remembers fixing breakfast in the big cookstove. The fire box was in the middle with a big oven on each side. It took a lot of biscuits to feed the Hephzibah family.

Grace's sister, Bessie Tyler Hampton, was a housemother at the Home for many years. A son was born to Bessie and her husband while they lived at Hephzibah. This little boy was named after his Grandpa Tyler and became a Free Methodist preacher just like him. Ordained in the Free Methodist Church in 1949, W. H. Hampton was destined to play an important future role in the life of Hephzibah.

Martha Braswell (now Downs) entered Hephzibah in 1918 when she was eight years old. She arrived in November with her sister, Ruby Lee, age 11, her brother, Herschel, age 9, and a younger sister, Christine, age 6. The Braswells were one of many families driven off the farm when the boll weevil ruined their cotton crop. Mr. Braswell tried selling Watkins products and did some carpentry work but he could not earn enough to support his family. He left for Jacksonville, Florida, to look for work. But he did not come back. Martha's mother did practical nursing during the influenza epidemic of World War I, but there was always the problem of finding someone to take care of the children.

Rev. Callaway recommended that Mrs. Braswell put her children in Hephzibah until she was in better circumstances. It was an answer to prayer. Adjustment to the Home was not hard, for the children had each other.

Martha has written of her memories of the four years she was at the Home. Sundays were special with white sheets for tablecloths in the dining hall. There was the meal when she tasted gelatin for the first time. Piano lessons were taught by a lady who came to the Home. On Memorial Day they all went to a cemetery for an observance. Other trips were to an artesian well and to a nursery.

One day Ruby heard that their mother was sick and she ran away to see her. She was punished by having to wash the "big house" outside. Martha remembers the day when she, too, was punished. One of the matrons, Mrs. Lingo, took her up to the bathroom after lunch and used a sewing machine belt to correct her!

She remembers the chinaberry trees and the canna lilies and other flowers planted by ladies from the Macon Garden Clubs.

One special person was Pearl Bigler, who strongly influenced Martha's spiritual life. She gave the little girl her first Bible with passages she had underlined and a personal message to her written in the front. As a result Martha was baptized and joined Tabernacle Baptist Church. "I was a very timid child," she writes, "but when I became a Christian I no longer needed to feel inferior. Jesus was my Lord and I was as important as any other person."

Uncle Willis Tyler and his wife stand out in Martha's mind. She remembers him as being tall and slender and she, a bit stout. They had morning and evening prayers with the children. Aunt Bettie is remembered as a warm and friendly person, while Mollie was more reserved.

Always there was work to do—churning cream into butter in a revolving barrel, picking bugs off the potato plants, peeling peaches after they had been put in the large wash pot outdoors so the peels would come off easily.

31

Annie Pearl Crawford (now Welsh) recalls her days at the Home. She arrived there in January 1914 at age 12 with a younger sister, Sarah. She remembers having church in the dining hall with Uncle Willis. The Free Methodist pastor also came to visit.

Annie Pearl did not help in the kitchen, but in a house called the hospital, which she recalls was the "old Hansen house." It sat farther back on the property and was equipped for use as an infirmary.

It was a constant struggle for the necessities, says Annie Pearl. Sometimes supper was a biscuit with syrup or apple butter. The children joined with Aunt Bettie and her workers in praying for needs to be met.

At that time around 70 children occupied the orphanage. The younger ones walked to Bellevue School, while the older ones went to a high school in town. Annie Pearl was the first from the orphanage to graduate form high school. She worked as Aunt Bettie's secretary for awhile after graduation.

The older girls, wearing white dresses, often went to sing in various parts of the state.

Board minutes for April 30, 1920, provide a glimpse of the financial picture, not only of the Home, but of the times. In the months since June 1919 income totaled $17,291. For food they spent $3,157; for fuel and lights $434; for telephone, $74; for labor, $2,764. Total disbursements came to $16,937.

In 1919 about two acres of the Hephzibah property were sold to the city water company, with free water for the Home as part of the transaction.

Aunt Bettie thought and prayed much about what would happen to the orphanage when she could no longer be in charge. Over 500 children had come under her care. She had labored against great odds, had felt she was "treading the winepress along," in her words. For a time in the earlier years she had been "a bed-ridden invalid." But her indomitable spirit continued to be the driving force. It was a source of great satisfaction to her that even in the dark days of World War I the Home's credit was sustained.

A letter written around 1920 gives an insight into the Christian character of this devout woman.

The Lord called me to give up all my plans and follow Him into orphanage work, not because I was the best woman He could find to finance an institution and mother and train orphan children, but because He saw this was the best means He could use to discipline me and develop my Christian character to where I could love God with all my heart and my neighbor as myself.

Many of her modern-day admirers are thankful God has other ways to accomplish those ends than the way He used Bettie!

She was ready to pass the torch to another. The board began looking for a way to perpetuate her work.

Chapter 5

Aunt Bettie Passes the Torch

Four men knelt under the pines at Hephzibah. They needed to know whether they, as representatives of the five southern conferences of The Wesleyan Methodist Church, should decide to purchase the orphanage.

Aunt Bettie had first turned to Rev. Callaway to see if the Baptist Church in Macon would take over Hephzibah. That was not possible. Next she asked the Free Methodists, her own denomination. They already had such a children's home. Then the Wesleyan Methodists were approached. The Book Committee, then the governing body, rejected the project. The northern churches were too far away, they decided.

The five southern conferences (North Carolina, Georgia, North Georgia, Alabama, and South Carolina) sent their presidents to look the property over. The president of the Alabama Conference, W. R. French, had inspected the property when the denominational committee met. W. D. Correll (South Carolina); E. M. Graham (North Carolina); and J. A. Wood (Georgia) met with Joe Lawrence, who was sent in an advisory capacity by J. J. Lawrence (North Georgia) who could not attend. Joe Lawrence, a prominent Wesleyan Methodist layman, who was already serving on the orphanage board, reported this meeting a few months later in *The Wesleyan Methodist* (Oct. 19, 1921).

Like the denominational committee, they were delighted with everything about Hephzibah. They saw the "magnificent, stately home on an eminence," the young pecan orchard, the "brick cow shed with its good cement floor and stalls fitted in the most modern style to accommodate fifty cows." Nearby were the dairy buildings and silo surrounded by "extensive pasture and woodlands." They beheld the "commodious dining hall, the neat baby cottage, the well-equipped hospital, barn and house for the farmer."

The men were well aware that they were not going to be charged the price the farm was worth. But they did not yet know the terms. They would be meeting with the present board of the orphanage right after dinner. Was it God's will for the southern conferences to take on this heavy responsibility?

They must pray until they knew for sure. Their earnest voices soon drowned out the murmur of the breeze in the pines above them. When they rose form their knees, the cloud of doubt had vanished. Bettie's torch had found willing hands.

The orphanage board minutes for May 5, 1921, reveal that "a tempting dinner served directors and visitors with the children of Hephzibah Orphanage preceded the directors' meeting." President Callaway called the meeting to order and gave an updated report of the search for those who would take up the responsibility of "perpetuating the Home along the lines by which it was founded."

After a free discussion by the directors, Bettie Tyler made the motion (passed unanimously) that the Wesleyan Methodist delegation be seated with the directors and the following proposition be made them, "that in the case they will take over the orphanage and its work and assume all financial obligations, amounting to $10,000, that we will be willing to relinquish present control and transfer property."

The final answer could not be given until the four men could bring this proposal to another committee.

Aerial view of the Forsyth Road property in early days

Original "commodious" house where senior girls lived upstairs and junior girls lived downstairs

On January 17, 1922, the group met again and the property was signed over. The cost? "Five dollars ($5.00) and other valuable consideration"—the $10,000 indebtedness. Graham, Correll, Wood, French and Lawrence and their successors were named in the legal document as the responsible parties.

In a letter to Rev. J. H. Lawrence, Bettie expressed herself thus:

While we know that God lives to answer prayer and there is nothing too hard for Him and for more than 20 years He has made ways where there were no ways and set tables in the wilderness, and supplied all our needs according to His riches in glory, there was always a part for me to do myself, and since you Wesleyans have assumed the responsibility that rested on me alone for so many years, I feel that it is my duty to tell you that it is time to pray that these children do not suffer for the necessities of life and that our credit which has been so long sustained here in Macon be not forfeited. . . .

The city of Macon and our contributors throughout Georgia are watching us closely. Everything good and nice provided for the orphanage recommended the institution to the public and thereby prove an investment.

Another good investment is a plenty of good wholesome food and wellmade genteel clothing. We get it back a hundredfold not only in the physical, mental, moral and spiritual development of the children, but in dollars and cents from the people who see we are doing something worthwhile. It is a wonderful opportunity you all have to recommend

Wesleyan Methodism and holiness to a gainsaying public. The thing most to be afraid of is grieving the Father of the fatherless by proving yourselves unequal to the momentous responsibility He has laid upon you. . . .

We feel this is only the beginning of Hephzibah's prosperity. We feel that you Wesleyans are going to unite and make this a model Home, that you are going to labor and pray and sacrifice to that end. You shall have my prayers and cooperation as long as I live and when I am dead I have an idea that I will come back as a ministering spirit.
Yours to do and dare and suffer for the orphans,
Bettie Tyler

This brave lady longed to instill her faith and courage into the Wesleyans! Surely God had designed more than to make Bettie herself a better Christian, as she thought. He had planned an institution that would minister to hundreds of children for years after Bettie's homegoing. In fact, she had the inner assurance that God was going to perpetuate Hephzibah Home until Jesus came back!

A lady from Ohio named Isabelle Whalen was chosen as superintendent of the Home when Aunt Bettie retired in 1922. No records have been found of the events of her administration. One history records a 1924 fire in the boys' dorm, but no account has been found of the repair or reconstruction.

According to *The Wesleyan Methodist* (Nov. 7, 1928) "on Monday, September 10th, about 12:40 p.m. in the Oglethorpe Private Infirmary at Macon, Georgia, the spirit of Miss Sarah Elizabeth Tyler left its frail home of clay and ascended to the God who gave it."

Chapter 6

Preacher Wood

While Aunt Bettie was praying for the continuation of the work of the orphanage, God was preparing a special man to become superintendent of the Home. Over in South Carolina the Wesleyan Methodist Church opened a new college called Central Wesleyan on October 15, 1906, with 19 students. Among them was John Archie Wood from Alabama. Two years later a young lady named Lella Rubye Dixon came to Central from southern Georgia.

The couple married in 1911 and pastored the Wesleyan Methodist church in Tuscaloosa, Alabama, for several years. In 1917 he became the first full-time president of the Alabama Conference. From 1920 to 1923 Rev. Wood served as president of the South Georgia Conference, driving a buggy and a little red mule from church to church and earning $300 a year, not always in cash.

It was during this time that the five southern conferences took the orphanage over. Rev. Wood's name was on the legal papers as president of the Georgia Conference. He had been in the prayer meeting under the pine trees.

In 1923 the call came asking him to see what he could do at Hephzibah. A caring man, John Wood was drawn to the challenge presented by the orphanage. Raised on a farm, he saw agricultural potential in the fallow land and unused barns.

Rev. J. A. Wood

The Wood family moved to Macon. At the orphanage the parents had a bedroom in the "big house." Their two older daughters, Olivia and Ruth, lived in the girls' dorm in the same building. Their son, Dixon, age five, moved into the barracks-like building where the boys stayed. Preacher Wood, as he is called by some even yet, had wooden lockers built along one wall of the boys' dorm so the boys could keep their clothes put away. Each locker was about thirty inches wide, four or five feet high and two feet deep and had a shelf at the top. Dixon remembers this clearly, over 50 years later!

Rev. Wood set to work to repair the dairy barn and the horse shed, and to start cultivating some of the land. The boys and girls helped put in a six to ten acre garden. Chickens and pigs were brought in. A dairy herd was started when Rev. Wood bought two or three registered Jersey heifers.

An old Dodge truck, with sides that looked like chain link fencing, was used for hauling. Children who performed well during the week got to go to town in the back of the truck with Mr. Wood on Saturday morning. They must have looked like little prisoners behind the wire sides of the truck, but they were excited about going to town.

The boys had their choice of looking after chickens or pigs. In the spring each boy had a big bucket in which the "litter" off the barn floors was carried out to the fields—an aromatic bucket brigade.

If a child wanted to plant a garden, he could have a plot of his own. Sometimes the young gardeners had vegetables to sell at nearby homes. Peaches were plentiful in Georgia. Preacher Wood took the truck and went to orchards to get "culls." Then all the girls pitched in to help can peaches, juice and jam in half-gallon jars. As the dairy developed they were soon enjoying their own milk and butter and sometimes, ice cream.

Another way Mr. Wood helped provide for the Home's needs was to cultivate acquaintance with wholesalers in Macon. Costs were cut on everything from hardware to jello.

At Christmastime Mr. Wood saw to it that every child got to go Christmas shopping. The younger children were given $.25-$.50 for their spree. The older grade-school boys and girls got $.50-$.75. Young teens received $1.00 or so and the juniors and seniors, $1.50-$2.00. These riches were exchanged at the "dime store" for the treasures they wished to share at Christmas.

One day a boy named Sidney came on the train from Butler, Georgia, and arrived at the Home wearing a tag with his name on it. Mr. Wood took this young teenager and trained him to manage the dairy. By this time a fine herd of registered Jerseys had been built up. The children "made over" every baby calf, spoiling them and loving them. But every spring buyers came from Tennessee or Virginia or somewhere to purchase some of the calves. A sad day!

Sidney was a busy, bright boy, taking ROTC training while in high school and art lessons from a lady near the Home. About the time the Woods left Hephzibah, Sidney graduated from high school and went into military service.

There were many happy times at the orphanage. Every summer all the children's homes in the area enjoyed Sunshine Day. Businessmen and clubs pitched in to provide this treat. The children were taken in cars and on floats in a big parade which ended up at Sunshine Park, a large play area at the edge of town, where they romped the whole day. This event was both anticipated and remembered for months before and after, so the excitement lasted all year!

One of the Wood boys remembers that the teens sometimes "paired off." "Once in a while we fellows would trade off sweethearts—especially if a knife, marbles, or a kite was included in the swap!"

The arrival of "missionary barrels" or boxes often proved to be a time of hilarity. Here would come a barrel with a monetary value placed on it. Rev. Wood must write out a voucher so the sending church or missionary society would get credit. The barrel would be opened and the clothing lifted out.

"Where did they get these things?" everyone asked. Some of them must have been stored in an attic for a long time. In fact some garments would have been appropriate for costumes in a Shakespeare play! The girls would use them to dress up in for "tacky" parties or for fun. But somewhere a church would get a voucher credit for $50 or $75!

Fortunately not all barrels and boxes held such unusable articles, for the children were dressed with donated clothing.

While the Woods lived at the Home, three more children were born to them: John Archie, Jr., in 1923; Mary Will in 1927; and Paul Baker in 1930. A few months before each birth, Rev. and Mrs. Wood moved to a house some distance from the "big house" or into a house off-campus to provide privacy for the blessed event.

The children loved to have the denominational leaders come to the Home (head men, they called them). Special services were scheduled in the dining hall when these important guests arrived.

Buck Fraley as a child   *John L. (Buck) Fraley*

Olivia Wood (Perry) remembers that her father was teaching her mother to drive a car while they lived at Hephzibah. One day she drove the model A car right through the garage and into the garden!

In 1928 the Fraley children arrived at Hephzibah—two boys, ages nine and eight, and two younger girls. Their father had died three or four years before. Mrs. Fraley kept her family together until she became ill. She had begun attending a Wesleyan church, heard about Hephzibah, and was able to get all four of the children into the Home.

After that, Preacher Wood had his hands full. John, the second Fraley boy, had been nicknamed Buck by his father before he died. Buck had energy to spare and made his presence known on the campus. It paid to be one of his friends, for he always protected his buddies.

When Buck misbehaved and was spanked by the superintendent, he would sometimes try to get even by picking on one of Preacher Wood's boys. One day Buck had the job of turning on the electric pump to fill the water tank. Toward the back of the property was a tall water tower with a shed below housing the pump. Every day, or maybe twice a day, the tank would have to be pumped full of water for the use of the residents of the Home.

Buck had turned the pump on and was waiting for the spillover from the tank overhead to let him know it was full. He saw John Wood, the superintendent's son, coming. Suddenly Buck remembered the spanking he'd gotten recently and decided here was his chance to get some revenge. Grabbing the boy, he pushed him into the pumphouse, locked the door and threw the key into the weeds. John began screaming for help.

About that time the tank began running over and now Buck couldn't get to the pump to turn it off. Needless to say, he was in trouble again!

After a whipping on another occasion, Buck and the other grade-school children were walking home from Bellevue School. Crossing the bridge over the railroad, Buck took John and held him, screaming, over the edge of the bridge. Some of the children grabbed John and others grabbed Buck and brought the prank to an end.

Clyde Putnam was Buck's best buddy. He slept on the cot next to his in the dorm. One morning about daylight a noise woke Buck up. It was Clyde crying.

"What's the matter, Clyde?" Buck whispered.

"I'm gonna get a whippin'," he sobbed.

Buck was puzzled. How could Clyde have done anything bad so early in the morning? Clyde never gave anybody any trouble.

"A whippin'! What for?" Buck asked.

"I wet the bed," Clyde said.

This called for fast thinking, because a wet bed meant a "whippin" for sure. Buck was out of bed pulling on his coveralls.

"Give me your sheet," said Buck.

Clyde took off the sheet and gave it to Buck, who stuffed it in his overalls. Out the window he went, down a drainpipe, hung the sheet on the line and was back in the dorm in no time.

"Make your bed, Clyde. No one'll ever know!"

All day at school, Buck and Clyde exchanged knowing smiles at school, gloating about their victory over the "system."

The flaw in their plan did not become evident until they came back from school and saw the sheet flapping on the line, a large water stain in the middle—and, of course, Clyde's initials on it!

Preacher Wood sent for Clyde, and Buck went with him. Before the superintendent could ask any questions, Buck said, "It was my idea." He didn't want Clyde to have to lie about it. So Buck got the whipping instead of Clyde. And the stage was set for another round of getting even!

In 1930 Mrs. Fraley, Buck's mother, married Rev. Walter Isenhour, and the four Fraley children went to live with them at Cherryville, North Carolina, where he was pastor. There were four Isenhour children already and then the new Mrs. Isenhour had three more. At age 13 Buck was second oldest of eleven children! He began "hustling" at an early age, making money at odd jobs. After working his way through military academy, he went to university one year and then was drafted. He became a captain of a company of combat engineers and served in Europe during World War II.

In 1949 Buck found employment with the Carolina Freight Company and worked his way to the top. The company is now the fourth largest motor carrier in the United States. Buck Fraley, a Christian layman, has established a trust fund in behalf of Hephzibah, which he loves for the contribution the Home made for two important years of his life. Mr. and Mrs. John (Buck) Fraley live in Cherryville, North Carolina, today and are members of the First United Methodist Church.

Over the years the superintendents and their teams of workers could not know the future impact of their lives and work. But they could be sure that in caring for children, they were touching tomorrow in ways that counted.

In 1929 Hephzibah trustees (southern conferences' representatives) voted to ask the Wesleyan Methodist Church to take over the orphanage, assuming liabilities amounting to $3000 and promising to meet the requirements of the founder in maintaining the work of caring for orphans.

In January of 1930 the Book Committee (comparable to the General Board of Administration today) agreed to the terms, and the transfer was made in "fee simple" just as Aunt Bettie had turned it over to the southern conferences in 1922. The orphanage was placed under the Home Missions Department.

Chapter 7

Depression Days

"**Y**ou're the one I want to come to Hephzibah as superintendent!" Preacher Wood looked earnestly into the face of D. L. Jones.

"Well, I don't know anything about it. I'm not a minister." Mr. Jones was puzzled.

"We don't need a minister, we need a businessman," replied the preacher.

The Depression was taking its toll at Hephzibah, as it was everywhere. The Home was going into debt. Preacher Wood had stuck by it for as long as he could. He was ready to go back into the pastorate.

D. L. Jones had been De Kalb county commissioner in Alabama for seven years. A farmer and owner of a grocery store, he was a careful businessman. He and his wife talked over Preacher Wood's proposal. It was a big step, not to be taken lightly. It would mean selling the business, a long-distance move and a whole new way of life. And what effect would it have on five-year-old Ginger (Virginia)?

The decision was made to accept the challenge, and they were invited to spend Christmas at Hephzibah. Mrs. Jones and Ginger left their home in Mentone, Alabama, and traveled to Macon. Mr. Jones needed time to wind up his business affairs and got to Hephzibah in January 1931.

Mrs. D. L. Jones, 1983   *D. L. Jones, 1955*

When the Jones family moved in, their quarters were on the first floor of the main building where the junior girls lived. Mr. Jones was horrified.

"This just isn't going to work," he told his wife. "I simply cannot share a bathroom with all these little girls!"

A call went immediately to a plumber in Alabama to come and bring the fixtures and fittings. A bathroom was soon installed and equanimity was restored in the Jones household.

Soon other changes were made. The outside stairway was torn down and an inside stairs put in. Now the senior girls didn't have to go outside to come down and use the parlor or the library. Mrs. Jones's father, Frank Shigley, came and built lockers for the senior girls to keep their belongings in. The children loved to have him come and were soon calling him Grandfather Shigley. Often his wife would fill a suitcase with homemade cookies and send them with him for the children. He donated hundreds of dollars worth of labor to the orphanage, and his presence made the place more like a home.

Mr. Jones had an addition built on the back of the dining room and installed large sinks with drainboards on each side. A big pantry was added where canned goods and other supplies could be stored. Mr. S. T. Coleman, a friend of the Home, gave a new wood-burning cookstove to replace the old burned-out one. And a shower and bathroom were put in at the back of the building.

Even with all his business acumen Mr. Jones had a struggle keeping the Home on top financially. Banks were closing. Money was tight. Yet the zealous solicitor, Mrs. Lucile Ernest, faithfully brought in $500-$1000 a month, contacting businessmen and well-to-do people in Macon and all over Georgia.

At that time the grade school children in the orphanage walked to school and came back for lunch. There were days when the children knew when they ate breakfast that the food supply was gone and unless

God intervened, there would be no lunch. The prayers of the children and the staff mingled in earnest petition.

Then it was lunchtime and the children would return to find food on the table. Perhaps a bakery had given day-old bread and pastries, or some other store or business had a surplus to give.

Brother Joe Lawrence brought great truckloads of produce and a lot of cane syrup, which the children loved on biscuits. Every morning the children had a breakfast of hot biscuits and homemade butter and syrup, grits and eggs, with milk to drink. At least there was one good meal to begin the day!

One day a man from south Georgia was hauling a load of frying chickens to Atlanta when his truck broke down right in front of the orphanage. He came in to use the phone and the buyers in Atlanta told him to try to sell them in Macon. He tried but failed.

"Could you use these chickens?" he asked Mr. Jones.

"We certainly can!" In fact they had been wondering what to do about meat.

What a busy place the Home was then! All those chickens had to be killed and cleaned. They had chicken fixed in every way they could think of. And they canned and canned and canned! They had chicken a long time—and not one can spoiled!

Mr. Jones asked that his salary be cut from $1500 to $1200 a year to ease the burden. He and the staff waited on God for the needs. At one time there were 69 children in their care. The income in 1930, the year before the Joneses arrived, had been $10,253 and the disbursements, $9,891. (Compare this with the 1920 financial report given in a previous chapter.)

They rarely bought clothing for the children. They wore what was sent in from the churches. It was discouraging to open a box or barrel and begin pulling out men's long underwear and women's foundation garments! Out to the old black boiling pot the underwear would go, to be washed and cut up for use as rags.

One day S. T. Coleman saw Mr. Jones when he came to town for the mail. "Mr. Jones," he said, "you seem to be carrying a heavy load. How are things out at Hephzibah?"

"Well, it's kind of slow going right now, Mr. Coleman."

"I'll tell you what I want you to do. Get your books together and come to my house one night this week. Tell me all about it."

Mr. Jones got his account books ready and drove to Mr. Coleman's lovely big house on College Street. When he walked in, his feet sank into thick carpet.

"Well, let's get right down to business. How much does Hephzibah owe here in Macon?" Mr. Coleman asked.

"I've got all the figures right here," replied Mr. Jones, opening his books.

Mr. Coleman looked them over carefully. "Some of these debts go way back there, don't they? Do you have it all totaled up?"

Mr. Jones, to be sure, was well prepared, for he knew Mr. Coleman's friendship for the Home. "Yes, here it is."

The wealthy businessman sat down at his desk and wrote a check covering all the outstanding bills that Hephzibah owed. When Mr. Jones came back with the news, there was a shouting time that night. Was Bettie Tyler there, a ministering spirit, rejoicing because once again Hephzibah's credit was sustained?

The Jones family was expecting their own addition and they moved into the farmer's cottage. Soon Ginger had a baby sister named Barbara. Everyone called her Bobbie and she became the darling of the orphanage. For all Bobbie knew, she had 65 (more or less) brothers and sisters! The Joneses kept Ginger and Bobbie under the same rules as the other children.

Scripture memorization was required of all the boys and girls. Each evening they sat at their assigned tables in the dining hall. Next to the Joneses' table were the senior boys' table and then the junior boys. On the other side were the senior girls at their tables and then the junior girls—ten tables in all. Each table had its turn to quote the Scripture verses they had memorized. Each person at the table had to quote a verse, or stand in a corner for ten minutes. If the child remembered a verse in that length of time and gave it, then he or she could sit down.

One night Bobbie hadn't learned her verse and her father sent her to the corner. This was more than the other little girls could bear. One of them hurried over to Mr. Jones.

"Oh, Mr. Jones, Mr. Jones, don't make Bobbie stand in the corner! She's too little! Let me go stand in the corner 'stead of her!"

He solemnly shook his head. "No, she had to do the same as the others."

"Oh, could I take her outside and teach her a verse?" the child begged.

Seeing the earnest face and the tear-filled eyes, the superintendent relented. Soon Bobbie and her friend came back in, Bobbie said her verse, and happiness reigned.

However much we may disagree with this method of teaching Scripture verses to children, the memorization had its effect. One night one boy quoted, "Be sure your sins will find you out." He added, "I know that's so, 'cause whenever I do anything bad, Mrs. Jones always finds out!"

Another boy's verse was "God will take care of you." His comment was, "I know that's true 'cause I stepped on a snake with my bare foot and it didn't bite me!"

When chores were done, the children enjoyed playing different kinds of ball or croquet. Mrs. Jones taught the girls to play hide-and-seek and other games she had played as a girl. The boys rode horseback on Brownie. Also included in the animal population were Beck and Belle, a team of mules that had been given to the Home. They pulled a farm wagon and hauled hay.

One day Miss Collins, the principal of the elementary school, came to Hephzibah bringing one of the boys. "I'm sorry, Mrs. Jones, but he has lice in his hair!"

The matrons stared in unbelief. They had an excellent housemother for the boys' cottage and she was so careful to see that the children under her supervision were bathed and their hair washed.

The boys' matron and Mrs. Jones took the boy and bean to examine his head. They found one louse. The matron uttered a little scream. "Oh, Mrs. Jones, you'll have to take over. I can't do this! I'm going to be sick!"

Mrs. Jones put disinfectant in water, washed the boy's hair and carefully combed it. No more "inhabitants" were found. When the rest of the children got home, what a dead-searching took place! From the oldest to the youngest, not a hair was left unturned!

Off to school marched Mrs. Jones the next morning to talk with Miss Collins. "We have examined every child in the orphanage and didn't find anything. I want you to call in the doctor and nurse and let them find out where this is coming from. It's not coming from Hephzibah!"

Dr. Williams was soon on the scene, assuring her, "Now, Mrs. Jones, don't you worry. I'll find where this is coming from." And sure enough, a little girl from a prominent family in Macon was found, whose head proved to be thickly populated.

And then came the apologies from teachers and principal, for the story had been whispered in every classroom that one of the Hephzibah children brought lice to school! Miss Collins even drove out to the Home to apologize to Mrs. Jones, saying, "This is the first time I've ever had to question anything about the Hephzibah children. They always come to school clean."

Mr. Jones expected the matrons to keep the children busy and happy. When someone misbehaved, the matron talked and prayed with the child. Many times the Joneses would take the big girls into the office and pray with them. They would break down and cry and no punishment was needed.

The spiritual life of the children was a prime concern. Sunday services in the dining hall featured visiting speakers (Home Missions Department Secretaries), such as T. P. Baker, W. L. Thompson, and Roy

S. Nicholson, as well as Foreign Missions Secretary E. F. McCarty. These men enjoyed being at Hephzibah. T. P. Baker told people about the touchdown he had made at the Home. He liked to play ball with the boys and once he fell down—that was his touchdown!

The old bus often took the children to the Free Methodist Church. They also had a good relationship with the Bass Methodist Church across the road from the Home. The Methodists would come to the orphanage when the children put on a YMWB program. Two of the main members of Bass Methodist were Mr. and Mrs. Davis. They asked Joneses to get a Wesleyan preacher and singer to hold a revival in their church. Rev. C. K. Gentry and Frank Dennard came and stayed at the Home and held a revival at Bass Methodist. The Hephzibah crew attended faithfully. It was a wonderful revival with many seekers.

A tiny baby girl was brought to the Home one day, granddaughter of a prominent doctor, who did not want anyone to know that his college-age daughter had given birth. The children were fond of the baby. Ginger and one of the other older girls took care of her. But the baby left the Home at six months of age to be adopted by a family in Alabama, who gave her every opportunity. The girl became an outstanding musician. Her mother never contacted her until she found out how talented she was. One day she came to see her, but the girl said, "You didn't want me when I was helpless, and I have no time for you now."

One little girl named Gladys was in the Home when Joneses came. The Woods told them the child had been found living with her mother in a cave near the Ocmulgee River. When she was found, her blond hair was matted and dirty and she was unkempt and simple-minded. Ginger took a special interest in her, fixing her hair until it shone like gold and taking her to school. Gladys learned to do a lot of things and really wanted to serve the Lord. Eventually she was taken to an institution called Gracewood in Augusta where she was trained and then was hired to work there.

Mrs. Jones remembers many of the children who were raised in the Home and she corresponds with some of them. Included are preachers, doctors, missionaries, nurses, pastor's wives, a conference president's wife and businessmen. One man, John Turner, a former Hephzibah child, owns two funeral homes. Of course, as in many families, not every child turns out like the parents wish.

During World War II, 19 boys from Hephzibah went into the armed forces. They wrote back and some of them told of the close calls they had. They felt it was the prayers of their family at the Home that kept them safe. One boy was wounded, but they all came back.

Perhaps the testimony of one of the "Jones girls" represents the feelings of many. Glendora Wiley, at Hephzibah from 1927-1939, writes:

"I have lots to be thankful for. It was at Hephzibah that I made friends and received special training that I have not forgotten. It was there I was taken in and loved and cared for as my father was not able to take care of me. They gave me a home when I didn't have a home.

"I was there during the Depression years, but I was small and don't remember the hard times. We were all treated like brothers and sisters. I'll always remember the Joneses, for they showed us love and took us on trips. They showed us and told us they loved us and if we had problems we could go to them and they would pray for us and with us and help us all they could."

When Rev. W. L. Thompson became Home Missions Secretary, his goal was to liquidate Hephzibah's original indebtedness, for $2,500 was still owed on the $10,000 debt that the five southern conferences had taken on in 1921. That goal was reached in 1936. It was suggested by Mr. Russell Baldwin that Wesleyan Sunday schools take a Thanksgiving offering for Hephzibah. This was done in 1940 with $1500 raised, and again in 1941 with $3500 raised. Wesleyan Methodists were rallying to the support of their children's home.

While the Joneses were at Hephzibah, many improvements were made. New equipment was bought and paid for, the buildings were remodeled and redecorated, and an intensive farm program was undertaken. A new bus was purchased in 1939. Hephzibah had come through the Depression with flying colors!

The Joneses had worked long hours for eleven years. Mrs. Jones had supervised the matrons and often served as matron. She had been dietician, helped with the cooking, taken the high school students to school, and done the secretarial work. By 1942, her health was affected and Mr. Jones told the board they must find someone else to serve as superintendent.

Mrs. Jones, now a widow, lives in Macon with her daughter, Virginia (Ginger), who is the widow of Berl Elder. Barbara (Bobbie) is the wife of Rev. Joe Phillippe.

Chapter 8

Yankee in Dixie

To replace Mr. Jones, the board located a man in Denver, Colorado, who was working with delinquent children. Wendell Campbell, an elder in the Kansas Conference of the Wesleyan Methodist Church, had been a pastor, a schoolteacher, and was interested in youth work. His wife, Vera, like her husband, a graduate of Miltonvale Wesleyan College (Kansas), was also a schoolteacher.

Hephzibah—yes, they had heard of the place, but didn't know much about it. How would a Northerner fit in? How would someone manage who wasn't a farmer? How would the staff and children accept a new superintendent?

The Campbells decided God wanted them in Macon. In November 1942 they headed south. They knew they were in a different culture before they ever got to Georgia. Somewhere below the Mason-Dixon life they stopped at a restaurant and were served something that looked like white cornmeal mush. Gravy was served with it.

"What is this?" Mr. Campbell asked the waitress, pointing to the unknown substance.

"Why that's grits, Sir."

Grits and gravy. The Campbells would eat a lot of that in the next five years!

Mr. and Mrs. Wendell Campbell in recent years

The new superintendent and his wife found there were a lot of things to get used to. One of them was the racial situation. In those "pre-civil rights" days, blacks were expected to "know their place." But Mr. Campbell was a Northerner—a Westerner, to be exact—and was still trying to figure the South out.

Two black women worked at the Home. One was head cook and one in charge of laundry, and both were faithful people. The cook came to work on the city bus and at the end of the day someone took her home, usually in the truck. One day it fell to Mr. Campbell to take the cook home in his car. He opened the front door for her on the passenger's side. But the cook didn't get in.

"We're ready to go now. You can go ahead and get in," he said.

But she held back. Finally she said, "Mr. Campbell, I think too much of you to ride in the front seat with you. I'll have to get in the back."

It would be many years before that mindset would change.

Gradually the Campbells "learned the ropes." While the Joneses were there, guidelines had been adopted for admitting children. In order to live at the Home a child had to be at least six years old and with one parent dead, be free from chronic disease and mental disorder, and not be "illegitimate." The child would be returned to his home when his parent remarried, or could be dismissed if he proved to have bad habits or when removal was necessary to the well-being of the Home and its ideals.

Mr. Campbell ran into problems with some of the children that his college and university textbooks had not prepared him for: one day a lady from the Department of Social Services in Washington came to check the Home out for some research she was doing. Mr. Campbell told her about some of the children with problems and she suggested that in addition to the medical attention the boys and girls received, they try to get psychological counsel. This proved to be helpful advice.

One of Mr. Campbell's goals was to get the Home licensed by the state. The Campbells did a great deal of research on other children's homes and their programs. Meeting the requirements for licensing took a lot of time, energy and money. For one thing, the state required that all the children sleep in single beds. So Mr. Campbell got rid of all the double beds and bought iron single beds. At last the requirements were met and Hephzibah was state-licensed.

Butchering time was fast approaching. Mr. Campbell had heard about this important event and he began to realize its significance.

Ino Sanders

"You know, Vera," he said to his wife, "I'm not going to have any status around here if I can't butcher a hog. They won't think I amount to anything!"

Ever the learner, Wendell went to town and bought an illustrated book on hog-butchering. Never was there a more diligent scholar. Prepared or not, he faced the dreaded day. He cut the pig open like the book showed him. To his relief the inside of the animal looked like the one in the book! But progress was slow.

The head cook took pity on the Northern city slicker and got her husband to come and teach him how to butcher. Before long Mr. Campbell could dress a whole pig in less than 30 minutes.

Out in the tomato patch one day Mr. Campbell was laughing with the boys as they pulled weeds. One of the boys said to the superintendent, "Mr. Campbell, you don't seem a bit like a Yankee to me!"

Wendell knew then that he had arrived!

A special person came to work at Hephzibah while the Campbells were there, a lady named Ino Sanders from South Carolina. She was a boy's houseparent and was well loved by children and staff alike. The Campbells cherished her as a wonderful friend.

Two other faithful women who worked as houseparents for many years during this period of Hephzibah's history were Esther Keesler and Mary Harness.

The Campbells had no children of their own until after they left the Home. Later Rev. Campbell served on the faculty of Miltonvale Wesleyan College.

Boys' dorm with dining hall below

Rev. and Mrs. Homer Rich and daughter

In the course of Hephzibah's history, staff and children had attended a Baptist church, a Free Methodist church, a Methodist church and had held their own services "on campus." Wesleyans deplored the lack of a Wesleyan church in or near Macon, and the matter of starting one was placed in the hands of T. P. Baker at the board meeting in January 1935.

The burden for a church in Macon was laid on the hearts of Rev. and Mrs. Homer Rich, who in the mid-1940's were pastoring in Noblesville, Indiana. Arrangements were made for them to go to Macon.

In May of 1947 Rev. J. R. Swauger, Home Missionary Department Secretary for the denomination, bought a 30-by-63-foot tent which was placed on lots purchased in west Macon about two miles from Hephzibah. This was not to be a church for the orphanage only.

Soon after the Riches arrived and were settled, they bought a two-story soldiers' barracks, tore it down and stacked the lumber on the church property. Much of this was "hard to get" material which was later used in the construction of the church building.

The president of the North Georgia Conference, Rev. H. A. Johnson, organized Rev. Rich's congregation as a Wesleyan Methodist church on July 11, 1947. In 1948 their average attendance in Sunday school was 43 and in 1949 it was 79. By that time they had a lovely brick church building valued at $20,000. Mr. Campbell was the first superintendent of Hephzibah to be a part of this new church, which was a church home for the orphanage for nearly 30 years.

Morgan Street Wesleyan Church in Macon

Chapter 9

Golden Anniversary

When interviewed in 1989 for the first edition, Rev. Edward Parker Buck, Sr. was the oldest living superintendent of Hephzibah at age 93. He died in January 1992. The Wesleyan Methodist Church leaders asked this preacher to leave the field of general evangelism and go to serve at the children's home. The Bucks took on this task in 1947.

Like other new superintendents, Rev. Buck found a lot to get used to. At the end of the first month he gathered all the financial papers together and had them audited. Then he sent a single sheet of paper, with the report, to the denominational headquarters in Syracuse, New York. No one had told him it was not done that way! He heard from them immediately. Why hadn't he sent all the papers? Everyone connected with the Church sent all their financial papers to Syracuse to be audited.

But Rev. Buck pled his case. Why all that bother? Why couldn't one sheet of paper do it all? Why not use local auditors? After due consideration the officials decided to make a change, and Rev. Buck's plan was implemented across the Church.

At that time Hephzibah's farm operation included the rental of a farm north of the Home property. Rev. Buck and the boys worked on that farm as well as at the Home, along with Mr. Parker Jones and Mr. W. J. Maw, hired as farmers. A Cub tractor was purchased, and that made the work easier.

Edward Parker Buck, Sr., 1961

L to R: Rev. and Mrs. Buck, Mrs. C. Slater, Mrs. Mary Church, Mrs. Lucile Ernest, Miss Ino Sanders (1949)

The superintendent's cottage (1949)

One day two little boys came to live in the Home. One, age 12, was feeling very lonely. Rev. Buck put his arm around the boy. Tears were in the eyes of both superintendent and orphan. "Joe, you'll be my boy from here on." Forty years later Rev. Buck was still moved when he spoke of this, for he felt that God had a special work for that boy to do. "I'm glad I lived to see it," he said. This boy's story is told in chapter thirteen.

In 1949 Mrs. Buck's health began to fail. The Doctor said to Rev. Buck, "You must get your wife away from Macon." It was with reluctance that the Bucks left the Home, for they loved working with the children.

A 1950 booklet about Hephzibah written by J. R. Swauger records these words by Rev. Buck:

> *One day while the problems of management were heavy, the calls from the outside many, the finances a real concern, and some of the inmates in need of correction, we were reminded by the Holy Spirit that we were not carrying on simply for the sake of the children, the Church, nor for self; Hephzibah was an Institution established, maintained and managed "For Jesus' sake."*
>
> *Just to keep the child for his own sake, profits, and comforts and to save him from the hazards of the world, is certainly worth consideration. It has its values, but is lacking in the more essential thing. Jesus will lighten the burden, cause men to respond, and promote interests, which otherwise would not be realized or worthwhile, if we do it for His sake.*
>
> *All during the life of Hephzibah there has been maintained a constant emphasis of spirituality. This has been foremost during all the years. The testimony of Mrs. Lucile Ernest, who has been faithfully working with the Home since about 1900, is, "These days seem like the days when Aunt Bettie Tyler began here; God still blesses like He used to."*

Surely Aunt Bettie's influence lingered and she was the "ministering spirit" she had foretold.

Two busy people living in Pennsville, New Jersey, came into focus next, as replacements for the Bucks. Rev. Raymond S. Taylor and his wife, Margaret, traveled 25 miles to Vineland to pioneer a Wesleyan Methodist Church there—the second church they had helped to build. Margaret had been teaching school in Deepwater, New Jersey, for 25 years.

When Rev. Swauger, Home Missions Secretary, approached the Taylors about being superintendent at Hephzibah, they were surprised.

Rev. Raymond Taylor

*The Taylors with Janet Revell
and "Cotton" Lane*

It took much thought and prayer to come to a decision to pull up roots and move to Macon, Georgia. This they did when they concluded that God was leading. "God won!" says Margaret.

Arriving at Hephzibah sometime in 1949, Raymond and Margaret began to learn from Rev. and Mrs. Buck just what was expected. Margaret writes, "It took us awhile to learn the children's names and dispositions, rules and regulations, the do's and don'ts."

After the Bucks left, the Taylors were immediately grateful for the good staff. Mr. and Mrs. Bennie Lane were in charge of the kitchen and turned out excellent meals. Mr. Lane also helped with farm work, which was extensive. The December 1949 board minutes report that the Home sold 200 pounds of milk a day, earning about $350 a month. The sale of eggs added to the farm income. That year 50 fruit trees and 5,500 strawberry plants had been set out.

Rev. Taylor helped the boys paint the barn. He rose each morning at 4:00 to supervise the milking, feed pigs, chickens, turkeys and other livestock.

Matrons working with the Taylors were Miss Mary Harness, Miss Ino Sanders, Mrs. Day and Miss Florence White. Mrs. Ernest was the solicitor, but money was coming in so slowly that the board of the Home authorized Mrs. Taylor to travel for solicitation of funds. She had never done anything like that before and had to pray much over it. But as she puts it, "God won again! I solicited as far down as Valdosta, Georgia."

For a special dinner one day a lot of chickens were killed and prepared. All the children and staff sat down to the chicken dinner. Suddenly one of the little girls burst out crying. "This was my pet!" Others picked up the refrain and refused to eat. The cooks put the chicken in the freezer to be served another time!

Hephzibah Home's fiftieth anniversary was set for Wednesday, June 28, 1950. A great celebration was planned. Margaret Taylor was the ideal person to help with an appropriate observation of this momentous occasion. She had written a program for a special event at the Macon church, calling it "When I Searched Heaven for You," and it was a great success. Her talents were now turned toward the golden anniversary.

Invitations were sent out, a program was planned, food was prepared and prayer was made for weeks for good weather and a successful day.

June 28 dawned fair and bright, and excitement bubbled from every corner of the campus, which bustled with activity. At 2:00 in the afternoon a photographer from the *Macon Telegraph* arrived to take pictures of the superintendents, Rev. J. R. Swauger, and Mr. Paul Haverfield, the juvenile probation officer of Macon.

At 2:45 the program began with a welcome from Superintendent Taylor to all "Board members, city officials, friends and past matrons and 'inmates.'" A response to this welcome was given by a member of the Exchange Club. Then Rev. Leslie Wilcox from Central College gave the invocation.

50th anniversary feast at Hephzibah

Play: "When I Searched Heaven for You"

Present for the occasion and participating in greeting were the mayor of Macon, a superintendent from a local sister institution, a representative from the churches and Rev. W. C. Lovin, who spoke for the Hephzibah Board. Another guest was Miss Nell Collins, principal of the elementary school the children attended.

The speech maker of the afternoon was Rev. Swauger, who talked on "Contributions of Hephzibah." Then the children sang while Mrs. Taylor accompanied on her accordion. Everyone enjoyed a barbecue supper with potato salad and ice cream and cookies while the Salvation Army band provided music.

"An unforgettable climax," according to Rev. Swauger, was the pageant presented at the close of the day. People were weeping by the time it ended.

Fifty years of service, touching the tomorrows of hundreds of children, had given Hephzibah Home an excellent reputation.

Rev. Taylor not only supervised the Home for three years, he was also pastor of the Macon church for one of those years. The burdens were heavy. They felt the pressing need for a new building. The November 15, 1950, *Macon Telegraph* carried a story on expansion plans. The golden anniversary contributions gave impetus to plans for a new 14-room, two-story edifice, for which blueprints had been drawn. But that's as far as the idea ever got. The construction cost of $20,000 was a forbidding goal when cash on hand was only $1,900.

Raymond Taylor became ill and began losing weight. Under doctor's orders he resigned and he and Margaret returned to New Jersey, where she got her old job back. Five years later Raymond passed away. Margaret, who later married Floyd Miner, is retired and lives in Largo, Florida.

Once again the Hephzibah board began to look for a superintendent. Dr. J. R. Swauger telephoned Rev. George E. Davis. A graduate of Marion College, Marion, Indiana (now Indiana Wesleyan University), Rev. Davis had extensive experience as a pastor in Alabama, Georgia, Tennessee and Indiana, and had also served as a prison chaplain and as vice president and president of the North Georgia Conference.

Rev. Davis agreed to go as superintendent of the children's home and arrived there in July 1951, shortly after the General Conference had transferred the Home from the supervision of the Home Missions Department to the denominational board of administration. Relieved to find things left in good shape by his predecessor, Rev. Davis turned his efforts toward improving the farm operation. The "pork program" developed until they produced all the pork needed for the Home. Milk production provided extra income, and bountiful gardens produced vegetables.

The Hephzibah group at church

Mrs. Lane, the cook at back of boys' dorm

Hephzibah staff L to R: Ella Cauthorn, Florence White, Miss Hinebaugh, Miss Slater, Miss Withrow, Mrs. Lane, Mary Harness, Ino Sanders, Bennie Lane, Margaret Taylor, lady in striped dress identity not sure, Clarence Cauthron, E. P. Buck, Sr., Walter Eastlack

High school girls and boys May 8, 1949
L to R: Lillian Lane, Patti Robinson, Beulah Hammock, Merideth Nichols,
Ruth Maw, Martha Newton, Voncile Edge, Betty Jones, J. B. Church,
Billy Joe Maw.

Junior girls with their matron, Mary Harness (center)
L to R: Frances Revelle, Gail Bradley, Amy Buck, Patsy Taylor,
Patti Robinson (girl on floor unknown)

Mr. Davis decided the older teens needed "social life." A dating program was set up for young people sixteen and older. Under the supervision of a matron the teens could pair off and meet in the library in the "big house." A supervised study hall period was also scheduled in the library.

During Mr. Davis's tenure the shop building was remodeled for use as a guest house where visitors could stay and workers could spend their days off when they did not leave the Home.

By this time the pressing need seemed to be for a home for the superintendent. Plans were made for such a building and when the

Rev. and Mrs. George Davis

The new house for the superintendent

Edward Parker Buck, Jr.

Home fell heir to estate money amounting to $12,000, it looked like a new building of one kind or another might soon become a reality.

In 1952 the Hephzibah board once more was looking for a superintendent. Dr. Swauger recalled meeting Ed and June Buck some years previously when they were visiting the older Bucks in a pastorate. Edward Parker Buck, Jr., in 1952 was working in insurance in Dallas, Texas. When he and June received the call, their minds went back at once to the time the older Bucks had been at Hephzibah.

"They loved it there," Ed remarked.

But would they love it too? They had two children: Amy, age six, and Brian, age four. The older Bucks had not had children living with them at the time they were at the Home. After much prayer Ed and June agreed to make the long move to Macon.

The problems and needs hit the young couple like a cold blast when they arrived in late 1952. New buildings were an urgent necessity, especially a house for the superintendent. A shed full of unusable donated clothing was downright depressing. And worst of all were all the clashes between staff workers.

The lack of privacy, the long hours, the desperate needs proved wearing—as they were to all who took this demanding job. It was a happy day when construction began on the house for the superintendent. Circumstances were more felicitous when the Buck family moved into the lovely brick cottage in 1953. The need for good workers was alleviated by the securing of Dorothy Allison in 1954.

By 1955 Ed and June, now expecting their third child, felt they had made their contribution to the Home and it was time to move on.

Chapter 10

Let Us Rise Up and Build

esse E. Towner had a warm spot in his heart for Hephzibah Children's Home. His mother had worked there as a houseparent and was now a secretary. But lately a strange thing had been happening to him and his wife.

"I just feel drawn to Hephzibah," he told her.

"Do you suppose God wants us down there?" she asked.

It didn't really make sense, humanly speaking. Mr. Towner was a supervisor at the Mercury Aircraft plant in Hammondsport, New York. He had no training for supervising a children's home.

They said nothing to anyone as their sense of a call grew stronger.

"If we hear from Hephzibah, we'll know it's God's will," they agreed.

One night they got a call from Ed Buck asking them to consider coming as houseparents. But that didn't seem to be the way God was leading. So they waited and prayed.

Then Rev. J. R. Swauger called and asked them to go to Hephzibah as superintendent and head matron. The Towners met with Rev. Swauger in a nearby town to talk it over. They knew God was calling. The drastic cut in pay was no consideration when they knew what God wanted them to do.

Arriving at the Home in February 1955 with their son, Richard, they settled into the superintendent's home and began to look the place

Mr. and Mrs. Jesse Towner and son, Dick

over. By this time the boys' dorm was showing its age. The plumbing and wiring were a disgrace. Time after time the bathroom upstairs made its presence known in unsavory ways in the dining hall below. Many times the tables and floor had to be cleaned up before a meal could be served. As if that were not enough unwanted moisture, when it rained, the water poured off the roof, formed a river, and ran through the door into the dining hall.

The furnace in the girl's dorm was old and cracked and emitted noxious fumes and copious clouds of smoke. The fire department often came to stand by when the "volcano" began to erupt.

The city and state health officials were extremely unhappy with the situation, and the Towners had been there only a few months when the buildings were condemned. They could continue to use them, but they had to get new facilities under construction speedily.

The Towners tried several times to draw up plans for a cottage that would be workable, economical and satisfactory to the state. But it proved to be a futile endeavor. Many times Mr. Towner, on his way into his office, paused with his hand on the doorknob and wondered, What am I doing here? It would have been so easy for them to leave and go back to New York. But the Towners were sure of their call.

Board minutes over the years show that action had been taken periodically to repair, remodel, redecorate, enlarge and otherwise make the existing buildings adequate. Inevitably, of course, new buildings would be essential. But for years it was the stuff dreams are made of. Now those dreams must be turned into reality, even though the Home was barely getting enough income for operating expenses.

Every morning after the children went to school, the staff gathered with the Towners for prayer in the superintendent's house. These people were at Hephzibah because God had called them. Concentrated, earnest prayer went up to God. If there were hurt feelings or any resentments or wrong attitudes among the staff members when they went to prayer, there were none when they finished. A sense of unity of purpose gripped them.

About six months after the condemning of the buildings, the staff agreed to pray a prayer of complete surrender. "Lord, we have tried every resource we know and nothing has happened. Now if you want the Home to continue, it's up to You. If You want to close the Home, it's all right too."

They were reminded of Aunt Bettie's convictions that God would keep the Home open until Jesus came back. Surely God would undertake in this crisis.

In 1956 Mr. Towner called Dr. H. K. Sheets, Secretary of Home Missions, and asked him to come two days before the scheduled meeting of the board of directors of the Home. (The 1955 General Conference had placed Hephzibah once more under the supervision of the Home Missions Department.) Dr. Sheets came and talked the situation over with Mr. Towner. Then the visiting Church leader took a tour of the buildings. Without a word, he looked them over carefully.

At the board meeting next morning Dr. Sheets told the members to go out during the noon hour and look at the buildings. When the board met after lunch Dr. Sheets said firmly, "Gentlemen, we *have* to do something!" Then they took action to appoint a building committee and to get construction started on new cottages.

The vote had no more than been taken when Mrs. Towner came to the door with a letter. "I think the board would want to read this," she said, handing the letter to her husband.

The letter stated that $4,000 had been set aside in trusts for Hephzibah Children's Home to use as soon as a building contract had been signed. It was the beginning of a series of miracles, some of which

Rev. and Mrs. W. H. Hampton and Lucile Ernest (center)

Senior girls' cottage

Junior girls' cottage

had been in the making for many years. The board, circumstances—and God—confirmed that it was time to "rise up and build" (Neh. 2:18).

Mrs. Lucile Ernest, not long before this, had been cited by the board and given special appreciation for 30 years of service as solicitor for the Home. During those years she had made many friends for Hephzibah. In 1928, because of her work, a man named Roy Nall Cole left one-eighth of his estate to benefit the Home. His wife was to have the interest from it as long as she lived and then $28,000 was to go to Hephzibah. Just weeks after the board action, word was received of the death of the widow. The money came at the very time the building program was getting underway.

Money gradually became available, but this in itself intensified the pressure on Mr. Towner (Mr. T, as he was affectionately called).

"We need a contractor and we need building plans," he told the staff at prayer meeting.

"And we need a pastor," someone added.

Only too true. The church was "in the hands of the conference president." The delegates went to conference, hoping to get a pastor but none was available. The conference arranged for two Central College students to alternate preaching on Sundays. A local Free Methodist pastor named Rev. W. H. Hampton, the grandnephew of Bettie Tyler, was approached by Mr. Towner and asked to help the church out on Wednesday nights. After a time the college students tired of the long drives and stopped coming. Then Rev. Hampton was asked to be supply pastor until they could find a Wesleyan Methodist preacher to come. Reluctantly Rev. Hampton agreed and then joined the Wesleyan Methodists in another year or so. His "temporary" tenure as pastor lasted until 1967—11 years!

To everyone's surprise and delight, Rev. Hampton turned out to be a contractor as well as a preacher and said he would be glad to help. Now they had a pastor and a contractor. Where would they get the plans? One day a state health department official stopped at the Home. "Mr. Towner, I think I have found the plans you need. They were used to build the cottages at the children's home in Savannah. Go over there and look at their buildings and talk with the superintendent. See if it's anything you can use."

They drove to Savannah as soon as they could and found the cottages to be ideally suited for their needs. They then went to see the architect. Would he be willing to sell them the plans? they wondered.

"We're through with those plans," he told them. "If you can use them, we'll give you the plans and the specifications."

Once more God answered prayer.

In 1957 construction began on the senior boys' and senior girls' cottages. The staff and friends of the Home prayed in the needed money. Both cottages were completed at a total cost of $60,250, and $40,000 of that was on hand. The Women's Missionary Society promoted a self-denial offering in the spring of 1958 which provided $6000 toward the remaining indebtedness.

As the new cottages were nearing completion, the senior girls and boys asked every day when they could move in. It was around

Central building (dining hall and offices)

71

Christmastime in 1957 when one evening after supper Mr. Towner said to Mrs. Allison, "Well, I think your house is ready."

The girls rushed to their dorm and began carrying beds, mattresses, clothes and all their belongings to the new building. Mrs. Allison had bought new bedspreads and curtains. Each room had two beds. The new cottage echoed with excited voices as the girls moved in.

Jeanette Revell stood in the hall and looked in at the lovely room she was to live in. "I never thought I'd have a pretty room like this!" she said.

The front door of each cottage opened into a large entry room. To the left was a hallway with six bedrooms, a bathroom and a utility room. One of the bedrooms was for the matron or houseparents and it had a private bath. (Mr. Jones would have loved it!)

The senior girls' new home was named the Lucile Ernest Cottage while the senior boys' house was named in honor of J. A. Wood and D. L. Jones.

The senior girls were much more contented after moving into the cottage, which afforded privacy and pleasant surroundings. It seemed more like a family, too. They could fix snacks in their kitchen in the evening. On Saturday and Sunday they made breakfast in their cottage.

The senior boys moved into their new home shortly after New Year's Day. But the living areas of both cottages were rather bare and there were no window blinds. The Towners prayed much about this. One January day they went to town and selected durable, economic furniture. They admitted to the store owner that Hephzibah received very little income in January, February and March. "We can't pay you until after March," they told him.

He replied, "Whenever you can get the money, you can pay me."

Then they shopped for window blinds. They called the man their "blind man." They told him the same story and got the same answer. But neither merchant had to wait until after March. Within two weeks money came in for both furniture and blinds.

Once the senior boys and girls had moved, the junior boys were put where the senior girls had been in the upstairs of the big house. The lower floor of the former boys' dorm continued to be used as the dining hall and kitchen. The Hephzibah staff and board pressed on with the building of the cottages for the junior boys and girls. Another WMS offering brought in $13,000 and the YMWB, $4000. The junior cottages were finished in 1960. Now all the children had adequate family-style homes.

Again, there was the problem of furnishings, and the staff prayed some more. One day a letter came from a family in Oregon. "This morning when we got down to pray during our family devotions, the Lord told us to send $50 for furnishings."

Money began to come in from people all over the United States.

One big project remained. A central building was needed for a dining hall, kitchen and an apartment for staff. This loomed as an even bigger undertaking than the cottages. They began drawing up plans and came up with one that would be serviceable. Later they modified the original plan and made the kitchen smaller to save money.

Mr. Towner worked with the contractor when he came to lay out the building. The "big house" had been torn down and the new central building was to be built on the site. Soon construction began.

One day the builders ran into a problem. The plumber came to talk to Mr. Towner. "The drain is supposed to go right in the center of the kitchen," he said, "but with the dimensions laid out, there's no way it can be in the center. That kitchen is five feet bigger than it's supposed to be!"

Mr. Towner's heart sank. He knew this would mean added cost—just what they wanted to avoid. When he phoned the contractor and told him, the man exclaimed, "It can't be! You and I both laid it out so carefully!"

"Bring your blueprints and we'll double-check it," Mr. Towner told him.

The contractor did and then shook his head. "Well, you're right. There's five feet more than there should be in the kitchen. No problem! I'll absorb the cost."

Wonderful! They would have a bigger kitchen after all.

One night during the construction Mrs. Towner woke her husband up at four o'clock in the morning. "Jesse, do you realize there are no windows on one side of that kitchen?"

"Yes, we couldn't put them in remember? We shortened the building to cut costs!"

"We've got to have windows in there!" she insisted. In the dark they made their way to the building site and measured. Sure enough, there was room for a two-and-one-half-foot window on each side of where the stove would be!

"Well, God is surely looking after us!" said Mr. Towner. "We make mistakes but God doesn't make any. I'll call the contractor first thing."

When he make the phone call, the contractor said, "It's a good thing you called today. Those walls are laid right up to window height. Tomorrow would have been too late! It's just as cheap to put windows in as to lay the walls!"

A real boost for the building program came with a Thanksgiving offering for the Home in 1960 that brought in over $32,000.

What a happy day it was when the new building was finished in 1962 and they could tear down the old boys' dorm and dining hall! The campus was beautiful with five brick buildings. Their friends in Macon marveled at the way God had answered prayer. One prominent man said, "It pays to have faith!" The new buildings were a monument to the faith of the Towners, Rev. Hampton, the staff, the board, the children, and to all across the church who gave.

Brother Hampton, pastor of the Macon church during this time, also saw God work in wonderful ways. When he began pastoring there, the church seats were only pine boards nailed together. Often people tore their clothes on the nails. Rev. Hampton sometimes had to pay for a new pair of pants because the disgruntled churchgoer thought the church was liable for torn clothes!

The Lord helped the people buy oak pews, which were installed in honor of board members, solicitors and others faithful to the work of Hephzibah through the years.

The pot-bellied stove that heated the church gave out. Rev. Hampton was able to get a plumber to install heating units, although he couldn't promise the man when he would be able to pay the $1000 it would cost. The Sunday after the heaters were put in, an old school friend of Rev. Hampton with his new bride came into the service and dropped in a roll of bills when the offering plate was passed. When the money was counted, they found two one-dollar bills wrapped around ten one-hundred dollar bills!

Sunday night altar services occurred regularly, and many Hephzibah children and young people became established Christians who are raising their families for the Lord today. Rev. Hampton was a tenderhearted man, often weeping as he preached. He loved the children and the children loved him. Jesse Towner says of Rev. Hampton, "He was such a friend to the children. He came out and played ball with them and had parties with them. When God made His choice for a pastor for our church, He made a good one. We thank God for Brother Hampton."

Among the godly workers at the Home during this time were Mr. and Mrs. Raymond Phillips of Kansas, who worked in maintenance and as houseparents from 1954 to 1968. The black cook, Bessie Smith, began working in 1955 and proved to be a nourisher of souls as well as bodies. She retired in 1972. Her daughter, Doris, took her place in 1977.

Mr. Ralph Batchlett from Pennsylvania was drawn to Hephzibah in 1954. Jesse Towner says, "God sent him to us. He was like a spiritual counselor to us. Back in those days when we were having difficulties and circumstances looked insurmountable, Brother Batchlett came to us. He was a real friend to the children and he used to come and walk with the younger children to Alexander IV School. Another morning he'd take the senior boys or senior girls to school in his car. He was a delight for the children—like a daddy. In fact, they called him Pappy Batchlett. He started sending birthday cards to the children regularly."

Although their length of service did not equal that of Mrs. Ernest, two men served faithfully to solicit funds for the Home. Rev. Lloyd F. Nichols served for over thirteen years in this capacity. Harold Artley was a solicitor for over seventeen years and brought great encouragement to the staff and children until his death in 1974.

Board members also gave long and loyal service. One of the earliest board members (under the Wesleyans) was Rev. W. C. Lovin, who gave 40 years in that position.

Many unsung heroes have been part of the Hephzibah team, with little compensation. All had the satisfaction of touching tomorrow through helping children, but their real rewards will come later!

One of the houseparents on Towners' "team" was Dorothy Allison, who looks back on 24 years at Hephzibah. Her story is told in the next chapter.

Chapter 11

24 Years as a Houseparent

orothy's Model A car chugged up the North Carolina mountain road. It was Sunday morning and she was out early, making the rounds to pick up boys and girls for Sunday school. Lucille Green, a little girl with pigtails, was watching for her and came running to the car. Lucille came with Dorothy for many years.

Through the years Dorothy Allison picked up many children. She watched some of them grow up and become part of the Clyde Wesleyan Church. She was as faithful as clockwork on her self-appointed rounds.

One Sunday she was sick. She tried to get someone to go and pick up two little girls. No one could go and there was no way to let the children know. Dorothy felt bad, for she knew the girls would be waiting down by the road, as they always did. Later the girls' mother told Dorothy that the children waited and waited. They would not give up until long after Sunday school time was past. Finally the mother got the little girls back in the house. The younger one said, "Well, it just must not be Sunday!"

Dorothy's old car was often pressed into service. She took young people to conference and to youth camp. She also taught an adult Sunday school class. But somehow her faithfulness to the church and her work for the Lord at Clyde Wesleyan did not satisfy her. She often prayed, "Lord, open the door for me to work for You full-time!" She would soon be forty and she hoped God would show her something before long.

One summer she took her usual carload of youth to conference. On the campground was a young lady from a children's home in Kentucky. She had pamphlets about the home. Dorothy picked one up and took it to her room. Lying across her bed, she read about the work in the Kentucky children's home.

A voice clearly said, "You could do that kind of work."

She raised her head and looked around the room, thinking someone was

Dorothy Allison

there talking to her. She lay back down, realizing God had spoken. Yes, I guess I could do that, she thought. But she did not sense a drawing toward the home in Kentucky.

Returning home that weekend, Dorothy was surprised to learn that Ed Buck and his wife were at church. He was superintendent of Hephzibah and he spoke in the church that morning. As far as Dorothy could remember, no one had talked about Hephzibah before at Clyde Wesleyan.

The Bucks were talking to the pastor at the door of the church when Dorothy left. Just as she went by, Mr. Buck said, "We need workers so bad."

Dorothy rounded up the children she had brought and headed down the river road. The words "We need workers, we need workers" kept sounding in her ears.

The Bucks were staying at Dorothy's sister's home. Her mother suggested she go and talk with them. When she got there and said, "I heard you need workers at the Home," they jumped up and grabbed her arms. "Are you interested?"

Dorothy agreed to think and pray about it. Many thoughts ran through her mind. I've never done this kind of work. I don't think I'd like to live in Georgia. My Sunday school class doesn't want me to leave, especially Marie (a new convert). She was on the point of telling Bucks she wouldn't come when the Lord said to her, "You prayed for an open door and the door has been opened. Are you going to enter it?"

She approached Marie again and she was reconciled to Dorothy's leaving. After putting out a fleece, Dorothy knew the assurance that it was God's will, and arrangements were made for her to go to Hephzibah in three weeks as matron for the senior girls. Then an urgent call came. "We need you to fill in for the junior boys. The matron has to leave tomorrow. Can you come today?"

Dorothy decided to throw things in the car and head for Georgia. On the way she stopped for gas. The young man servicing her car said, "Are you a missionary?" For Dorothy it was further confirmation of God's leading.

It was a good thing she felt it was God's will. Nothing else would have prepared her for what she stepped into when she walked into the boys' dormitory at 11:00 that Saturday night. Fifteen boys, ages 6 to 11, were sleeping in iron single beds in a large room. On their lockers were the boys' names. The departing matron left her without a clue!

What an experience to get 15 boys ready for church the next morning! The senior boys were in the same building. Dorothy got the younger ones dressed and set them on a bench in front of the dorm. Along came the big boys and held them up by their heels. Hair was mussed and shirt-tails were out!

She mothered the junior boys for a month before she got to go to the senior girls' dorm in the "big house." She thought, Now I'll get to do the job I really want to do!

She carried her belongings up the stairs and walked into the big dorm room with the familiar iron beds circling the walls. She couldn't remember seeing a more depressing sight. Dirty wallpaper covered the walls. In one corner was an unpainted partition screening the "bathroom." A huge old-fashioned dresser stood nearby with a large mirror. The bare windows were painted partway up for privacy. The finishing touch was a great dark splatter in the middle of the floor where a bottle of ink had been dropped.

Well, at least my girls will be a bright spot, she thought. But that was the most depressing thing of all! The eight senior girls ranged from early teens up to 17. She smiled warmly and introduced herself. Cold stares greeted her.

"Tell me your names."

Their flat replies puzzled Dorothy. But in the days that followed she bent every energy to winning them over. Gradually she learned that they had "run off" the former matron and they were going to see how long it took to run this one off. In fact they had been without a matron for sometime. Mrs. Hervie Towner, houseparent for the junior girls downstairs, gave only general supervision.

Dorothy discovered that this leadership gap had been filled by Dora*, who had ways of getting the other girls to do as she said. When Mrs. Allison told the girls to clean their lockers, Dora came along and told them something different. One of the younger girls, Rita*, seemed inspired by Dora to be defiant.

Dorothy agonized before the Lord. "You've made a mistake, Lord. You've called the wrong one. They don't like me."

*Not real name

Old house where girls lived when Mrs. Allison came as housemother

She heard the unmistakable answer, "If I'd wanted someone else, I would have sent someone else."

Opening her precious *Streams in the Desert*, she saw right at the top of the page, "Be thou there until I send thee word." And beneath it was this poem:

I'll stay where You put me,
I will, dear Lord,
Though I wanted so badly to go.

"Then You'll have to give me more grace, Lord!" she prayed. She had been taking her problems to Mr. Buck, who would say, "You work it out." After her time of prayer and assurance from the Lord, Dorothy knew she had to be in charge. Dora was going to have to take a backseat. She squared her shoulders and walked from her room into the girls' big dorm room. Rita picked the wrong time to misbehave that day. As Dorothy walked into the room she thought, OK, this is it!

"Come here," she said to Rita. "I don't want to do this, but you have forced me to." She took the surprised girl into the matron's room and used a bolo paddle on her. When she turned to leave the room, there stood Dora. This is no time to back down, thought Dorothy. Looking the older girl in the eye, she said, "You come on in too if you want some. I can take care of you too!"

That was the turning point. The undaunted matron told her family of girls, "Now I'm going to tell you girls, I want to love you and I want to help you. The Lord called me here and you're not going to run me off!"

She looked for ways to help the girls. When Dora told her she had to do a home project for school, Mrs. Allison had an idea. "Dora, if you want to fix up our room, I'll pay for it and you can get credit."

Using old sheets and eyelet trim, they draped the big old mirror and covered the ugly bathroom partition. Curtains for the windows, paint for the floor, a dressing table with lamps—what a transformation! The girls were thrilled and Dora got an A-plus!

Then Dorothy began planning to take her girls on a trip. The children at that time rarely went anywhere except to school and church. What better place could she take them than to her home in the beautiful hills of North Carolina! Mr. Buck let her take the station wagon. The eight girls spent four days sightseeing and enjoying home cooking. Dorothy found that getting the girls away from the Home opened the door to a closer relationship.

When the senior girls returned with glowing reports, the junior girls clamored for their turn. Mrs. Allison was their housemother part of the time.

"If I can get a car, I'll take you," she told them. "You know I sold my old one. You must help me pray that I can get one." So they prayed faithfully every night.

She had been going back home by bus when she had a weekend off. But the long bus trips left little time for visiting. A car would be nice. But on a salary of $30 a month, how could she buy a car?

Her brother-in-law had a green 1954 Chevrolet, practically new, that he was driving. When she saw it she said to him, "Why don't you keep that car? Don't trade it off until I can get some money. I'd like to have it." But she knew it wasn't possible.

On a later visit home she saw he still had the car and expressed her wish again. To her surprise, her brother-in-law said, "You can have it and some extra money besides!" He pointed to a vacant lot next door. "Your daddy would give you that lot if you'd ask him. He's given lots to your sisters when they got married. Then you can trade the lot to me for this car and I'll give you $400 besides!"

And that is how Dorothy came driving up to Hephzibah in a new car. The girls swarmed around her. "Whose car is it?"

"It's mine! My two fathers gave it to me—my earthly father and my Heavenly Father!"

She put 150,000 miles on it, including a trip with the junior girls, and never had any trouble with it. When it got too old, she traded it to her nephew on a 1964 Chevy. He brought it to her and when he drove the "well-behaved" '54 out of the driveway, the muffler fell off!

God not only provided cars for Mrs. Allison, He answered the prayers of the staff for food. At one desperate time they all prayed

81

earnestly. One day she looked out the long windows of the big house and saw a car drive up. A preacher got out and called the boys to come. Opening the trunk he began to load them up with food to carry in. Dorothy watched with tear-filled eyes.

One summer they needed jars and sugar for the yearly canning. The senior girls helped the cook, Mrs. Breedlove, with this big job. Just in time, here came cases of jars and big sacks of sugar. The "revenuers" had taken the supplies from a moonshiner's still and decided to bring them to Hephzibah!

When people sent boxes of clothing the Home sometimes had to pay postage—only to open the box and find rags, ugly black dresses, or other unusable articles. Dorothy thought of what the children needed and cried as she stared at the contents of the box.

Then she got an idea and suggested to the superintendent, "Why don't we get a missionary society to take one child and take care of it. They could write to them and send pictures."

The idea took hold. Missionary societies "adopted" children. The Home sent clothing sizes and needs and suggested money be sent to buy shoes. It was a workable plan that made a wonderful difference in the self-esteem of staff as well as children. The method is still in use today.

Before that time, however, God did supply needs in amazing ways. One of the girls named Joan Joyner was about nine years old when one Sunday she came to see Mrs. Allison who was in bed with Asian flu. Dressed for church, Joan stood by her bed.

Joan stuck out her arms and her coat sleeves were up near her elbows. "Mrs. Allison, I've just got to have a new coat," she said.

"I know you do. I'll pray about it while I'm lying here this morning," Dorothy replied. Then she called Mrs. Towner and asked her to help pray.

That afternoon a lady came and brought a beautiful coat with brown and green flecks in it. "My little girl has outgrown this," she said. "I thought maybe you could use it."

It fit Joan and looked lovely with her auburn hair. A registered lab technologist today, she still talks about her miracle coat.

In the fall of 1955 all the children were outfitted for school except Billie, who was a very slender girl and hard to fit. Prayer had been made for this special need. A few days before school was to start, a box of clothing arrived with an ample supply of summer and winter clothing— all of it just Billie's size and exactly the right colors to suit her blond hair. Not a seam or button had to be changed to make them fit!

One year Mr. Towner was concerned that the senior boys have new sport coats. Two of the boys had such shabby coats. Just before Christmas a lady brought six coats, like new, that her son did not need. Two of them fit those boys perfectly.

One year Dorothy had a tax bill of about $18, which was due in December. Her money had gone for doctor and medicine. She prayed and prayed about that tax bill. One day one of the workers had to go to town and Dorothy offered to take her. As she drove down the street, she noticed a dollar bill fluttering in the breeze near the curb. Stopping the car, she got out to pick it up. It was a twenty-dollar bill! The Lord whispered, "There's your taxes!" She looked all around to see if someone nearby might have dropped it, but on one was in sight. She decided it was like Peter who got his tax money from a fish's mouth!

On another occasion she owed a bill for $40. She often prayed with Bessie, the black cook, and they shared each other's problems. So they got down and prayed about the $40 debt. Afterward Dorothy went over and got her mail. In it was a letter from Lucille Green in Clyde. Now grown and married, she was the little girl in pigtails that Dorothy had taken to church so many years. Why would she be writing to me? Dorothy wondered. Opening the letter she found a check for $50 and a note expressing appreciation for her and her work. She ran and grabbed Bessie and they rejoiced together. She remembered the scripture, "Cast thy bread upon the waters. . . ."

One Christmas was a memorable one for the Kelly sisters—Betty, Shirley and Wilma. Their mother and sister had died of tuberculosis and their father and brother were in a sanatorium. The girls had not seen them for a long time. After the gifts had been passed out that Christmas morning, they all went to the dining room for breakfast. The girls stayed afterward to help clean up, and Dorothy went back to the dorm. Parked in front of the house was a car with Mr. Kelly and his son inside.

"Oh, come in quick!" she said. "Let's surprise the girls!" She took the father and brother in and had them sit by the Christmas tree. When the girls came, she said, "There is one present I haven't given you yet." She took them in to see their family. What a joyful time it was for all of them. The father did not live long after that.

In Mrs. Allison's early days at Hephzibah there were few recreational choices. Staff and children made their own fun, and Dorothy was usually in the middle of it. During the years when Towners were there, Dorothy and Mr. Towner traded off practical jokes.

Someone had given a goat to Hephzibah and it wandered around the campus. Sometimes people in the "big house" saw the goat standing on the porch staring in the long (vertical) windows. One night Mr. Towner, in a playful mood, decided to "play goat." Crawling to one of the porch windows, he ran his hands over the window screen and gave a yell. Mrs. Allison jumped and screamed with fright. When she saw who it was, she yelled, "I'll get you back!"

She had a gadget which she called a "voice box" which could be squeezed to produce a cow's moo. If it was shaken and squeezed, it sounded like a goat. One misty evening she put on her raincoat and concealed the voice box under the coat. She went to the superintendent's house, got close to a window, and squeezed and shook the box. She could hear the Towners wondering what the noise was. She went back to the big house but she wasn't satisfied. Back to Towners she went, knocked on the door, and told Mrs. Towner she needed some nylon hose for her girls. While Mrs. Towner went to the attic where the supplies were, Dorothy saw Mr. Towner in another room and she squeezed and shook the box.

"There's that noise again," said Mrs. Towner, coming into the room.

"I think it's that old goat," her husband said.

"Let's go find it!" suggested Dorothy.

They all went outside to look, with Dorothy squeezing the box when Towners were away from her. The sound brought them back, still looking. On one side of the house was an opening to the crawl space. Dorothy made the noise again as they were near the opening.

"It's under there!" Mr. Towner called triumphantly. Down on his hands and knees he went to look in, saying, "Baa! Baa!"

It was too much. Dorothy began to laugh and brought the box out to show the superintendent how she had "gotten him back."

Fun-loving Dorothy got still more mileage out of this prank by writing a poem titled "Hepsi Goat."

Here's a little poem that's wrote
About the famous "Hepsi Goat."
The things he does is quite a fright,
Because he roams around at night
To peer out windows and around the doors,
Behind the hedges and under the floors.
He makes a funny "baa-ing" noise
That tickles all the girls and boys.
It makes the workers shout with glee
To see him down on bended knee
And with a very serious air,
Search for a goat that isn't there.
Now so you won't be led astray,
There's a few things I'd like to say.
The "Hepsi Goat" is Mr. T
Who really is a sport, you see.
That's why on him we've pulled our pranks
And for his sense of humor we give him thanks.
We'll miss him when he goes away,
And hope he'll come baa-ck to see us someday.

After this Mr. Towner began to receive all sorts of cards with goats on them and miniature goats of all kinds—addressed to him in care of Hepsi Baa Home!

After 24 years as houseparent, Dorothy retired in 1978 and went home to care for her mother. Her long tenure in the senior girls' cottage guaranteed her a large family of "grandchildren." Many of her girls write to her, go to see her, give her presents, and phone her at her home in Waynesville, North Carolina. In her billfold she carries many pictures of her girls and their families.

In the fall of 1988 when Dorothy was visiting the Home, one of her girls, Thelma Joyner Shepard, who lives in Macon, brought one of her teenage daughters to see her. As they had often through the years, they began recalling memories. Thelma was one of the junior girls when Mrs. Allison went to the Home in 1954.

"I remember my first meal when I got here. I came when I was seven," Thelma said. "They served liver, which I hate, and we had to clean our plates. It took me an hour to eat it. I never fix liver or bread pudding or rice pudding. I had my fill of them at Hephzibah!

"I remember Miss Carson reading to us five junior girls *Little Women* and *Five Little Peppers*. I was the youngest of the girls, but I soon became the leader. Whenever we played school, I was the teacher.

"When guests came, we were supposed to line up to greet them. One time Mr. Towner was bringing visitors through and when he got to the junior girls' dorm, no one was there. 'Where are the girls?' he said. 'Well, you can look around. Here are their beds. Here is where they put their dirty laundry.' He raised the lid of the large laundry bin and there were all five girls inside!

"Christmases were just unreal. We got enough presents to last all year. My first Christmas in the 'real world' was a disappointment. It was hardly anything compared to Hephzibah."

After graduating from high school in 1965, Thelma attended Central Wesleyan College for two years. In 1968 she was junior girls' houseparent at the Home and then soon married. She and her brother planned a double wedding, which took place in the Hephzibah dining hall.

Mrs. Allison helped several of her girls plan their weddings and sometimes traveled to other states to attend weddings. She has touched tomorrow in uncounted ways.

Chapter 12

The Sixties

Newark, Delaware, was home to the Weavers at the time they became interested in Hephzibah. Charles (Bud) Weaver drove a fuel truck for southern State Co-op. Their pastor, Rev Norman Handy, had a special interest in the Home, since his mother-in-law, Mrs. Floyd Leh, was a houseparent there.

In 1962 the Weavers stopped by Hephzibah on their vacation. Bud fell in love with it. "I'd like to come here some day," he said. A few months later word came that the Towners had resigned. Pastor Handy called Dr. Phaup who called the Weavers. Bud went to Marion, Indiana, for an interview and then to Hephzibah for a serious visit. Within two weeks, their house and furniture were sold. They said good-bye to Newark and with their three children, headed for Macon. Barbara was eleven, Rodney, six, and Ronald, four.

When the Weavers drove up the muddy road to the Home that cold rainy day in February 1963, they were welcomed warmly by the staff and given a delicious meal. In the days that followed they found a lot of work waiting to be done. The central building was being completed. A pile of rubble marked the spot where the last old building had been torn down.

Red mud everywhere! That was one of Weavers' first impressions. They began to dream of landscaping the campus and putting in blacktop drives, sidewalks, and parking and play areas. Another obvious need was new beds. The children were sleeping on old sagging mattresses on ancient peeling bedsteads.

The sixties proved to be a transition period. Traditional concepts were being challenged across the Church as well as society in general. The board of the Home reluctantly permitted a TV set in each cottage, to be carefully monitored.

Mr. and Mrs. Charles (Bud) Weaver

The Weaver children merged into the life-stream of Hephzibah with ease. Rodney was just the right age to enjoy having so many playmates. With no playground equipment the children devised many activities. The younger boys enjoyed a sandpile under the shade of a big pecan tree. Mixed with red dirt, the sand gave the children a colorful look by the day's end. One day the boys took flat pieces of cardboard and slid down the grassy hill in front of their cottage. They rode ponies and played "Tarzan" and "Army" in the jungle (woods). Rodney enjoyed talking to Dorothy Allison, who joked with him in her appealing colloquialisms, such as "doohickey" and "thing-a-ma-jig."

One of the Weaver's newsletters also mentions a day each August when the children enjoyed the Sunshine Special, a "modern version" of the Sunshine Day which was such a trend back in the '20s. In the 1960's the Sunshine Special was "sponsored by a civic organization for all the children's homes in Macon (six), and where they get to eat all the ice cream and drink all the lemonade they can hold."

The Weavers, like other superintendents, planned trips to churches and at least one district conference each year to present Hephzibah and raise money. Response was rewarding and encouraging as churches and individuals gave sacrificially. They reported these special gifts in their monthly newsletters.

"We shall never forget the Smyrna, Delaware, church for their sacrificial giving to furnish a water cooler for the senior girls' cottage."

"The Northside Church in Atlanta, Georgia, gave us money to screen in the back porch on the central building. . . . Money came in for an attic fan for the dining room. The building that was almost unbearably hot last summer is much more comfortable this year."

"Two churches gave $100 for playground equipment."

"With the offerings we received on our tour in Indiana, we were able to purchase two heavy-duty lawn mowers and finish our projects of new beds for the girls' cottages."

In January of 1965, the YMWB took "landscaping and blacktopping" as their project. The churches presented this in various ways. One visitor at the Home took a pair of Mr. Weaver's old boots covered with red mud to show their people. Several took home jars of red mud to use on posters or in some other way to dramatize "Operation Facelifting."

In the summer of 1965, the children got their playground equipment. An offering from Trainer, Pennsylvania, along with other money, provided sturdy secondhand swings, see-saws and monkey bars. By that time they also had new beds for the boys.

So it went—a constant reliance on God and the Wesleyan people across the country.

Spiritual concerns were ever present. The October 1964 newsletter reports "a wonderful revival at one service in the Macon Church last month. . . . We still feel the results of those victories as we see the changes in the lives and attitudes of some. We also feel more strongly than ever the power of Satan as he tried to discourage our young people and cause them to give up the wonderful experience they had."

The December 1964 *Wesleyan Missionary* carried testimonies from six of the children and young people. Eugene Bradley, age 18, speaks eloquently in testimony of how God used Hephzibah: "I'll try to tell you how much a Christian home has meant to me. I won't leave Hephzibah the way I came in. I love the Lord and He means the world to me. When I leave here He will go with me. I came to Hephzibah when I was five and I am now eighteen. Next year, after graduation from Lanier, I hope to go to Central."

But the reports weren't always so bright. In one newsletter the Weavers wrote: "There are many things that happen around a children's home that we are tempted to worry about. Why do the workers have so much trouble with misunderstandings, discouragement and feelings of uselessness? Why are we constantly criticized from all sides? Why do the children become seemingly indifferent to the message of salvation and get so anxious to leave and get out into the world? Why are they so quick to make fun of those who try to live Christian lives and condemn those who stumble and fall? We don't always know the answers to these questions and if we continually wondered about them, we would soon give up in despair. But we are thankful that we can take everything to God and leave it there."

At last the blacktopping and landscaping were completed. What a wonderful difference it made! The children and the floors were so much cleaner. A horseshoe drive connected the Home with the highway

Kathy Reece

and there were parking and play areas. No more riding bicycles through red dirt paths.

One of the children in the Home at this time was Kathy Reece. Years later she wrote:

In August, 1961, I arrived at Hephzibah Children's Home. I was eight years old and going into the third grade. Rev. J. W. Stiles, my pastor, had been instrumental in my coming to the Home and also actually brought my brother, Larry, and me. My parents were separated at the time so my mother was working hard at a mill to support my brother, me, and two of my sisters who are deaf and had to be sent to a deaf boarding school. At times I was shuffled around to various aunts, uncles and grandparents to stay. When I came to the Home, I received good food, plenty of clothes and a permanent roof over my head. I also had a Christian atmosphere to grow up in with a Christian staff and regular church attendance. . . .

I met and dated my husband, James [Shepard], while living at the Home and through my influence and others like Mrs. Allison and the Home he also became a Christian. With Mr. Joe Neyman's help and an anonymous donor I was able to attend Central Wesleyan College for two years before I left to get married in 1973. Now I have three beautiful daughters and a loving husband. . . .

I am so thankful Hephzibah Children's Home was here in 1961 and I hope it continues to be here for other children.

Kathy and her family live not far from Hephzibah and she often volunteers her time for work at the Home.

In August 1964 Lucile Ernest suffered a stroke and Hephzibah provided for her care in a rest home. This dedicated servant gave 54 years of her life to the Home as houseparent, teacher and solicitor. Someone said of her, "She traveled until her feet wore out and then she wrote to those who contributed until her hands gave out."

She went to be with her Savior in October 25, 1964, the day after her 87th birthday. At her funeral a tribute from the Hephzibah family, written by Dorothy Allison, was read.

"As unknown, and yet well known, as dying and behold we live,
As sorrowful, yet always rejoicing; as poor yet making many rich;

As having nothing, yet possessing all things" (2 Cor. 6:9-10).
Unknown to books and halls of fame, or speakers on the air,
But the Hephzibah family knew her well and esteemed her
*   sweet and fair.*
Dying to all that earth could yield, or this life could impart,
But living in the love of God, living in many a heart.
Sorrowful when seeing sin abound on every hand,
Rejoicing still that we may rest at last in heaven's land.
Poor in money, poor in goods, but giving of her best,
That all of us could dress and live "as good as all the rest."
Having nothing, no fine clothes, nor lovely home, nor gold,
But still possessing love and friends and God—all wealth
*   untold.*
She's gone now to her great reward, to heaven bright and fair
To ever be with our dear Lord. Let's prepare to meet her there.

Through the years, Mrs. Ernest and a host of other dedicated workers and faithful supporters had made Hephzibah a place of which Rodney Weaver later wrote, "I remember learning that love is the greatest thing in the world."

Mrs. Lucile Ernest

91

From Orphan to Superintendent

943—a year of tragedy, a year of war. But one's personal tragedy eclipses national disaster, as the small moon shadows the huge sun. For the Neyman family in Chattanooga, Tennessee, 1943 was the year when their husband and father died. Life had never been easy but it became even harder. Mrs. Neyman worked long hours and made daily sacrifices to provide for her five children. The two older girls quit school and got jobs to help support the family.

Fear clutched the children's hearts when they learned that their mother had cancer, and in the spring of 1948 she died. It seemed to Tommy Joe and Lavern that their world had fallen apart. Their oldest sister was married by this time. The other sister married a month after the mother's death. The oldest brother, age 15, decided to go out on his own.

When the relatives gathered in for the funeral, the big question in their minds was, what do we do with Tommy Joe and Lavern? The next six months were a nightmare for the two boys, ages 12 and 10. Bounced from one relative to another, they were lonely and confused. In their trouble they became close friends. Joe protected his younger brother and they both stood up for each other.

When school started, the boys went to Rossville, Georgia, to live with an aunt. Another strange place, a new school, and that awful feeling of not really belonging.

That dreadful year of 1948 came to a terrible climax on the night of December 30. Their aunt made an announcement that sent a shock of fear through the hearts of Tommy Joe and Lavern. "Get your things ready. You're going to a children's home in Macon, Georgia, in the morning."

The boys did not sleep much that night. What would it be like? How would they be treated?

The fateful day dawned cold and cloudy. The boys traveled with their aunt and cousin to this place with the strange name—Hephzibah. As the car came up the drive, the boys stared at their new home. A big white house with a large porch, another white building, a small house, and children here and there. A lady came and took them to the man who was in charge. His name was Rev. Parker Buck.

The two new boys saw children coming up to look at them, and Tommy Joe and Lavern stared back. Soon their few belongings were carried from the car to the boys' dormitory. The main floor was a big open room with a partition down the middle. On one side lived the big boys and on the other, the little boys.

Their aunt helped them put their clothes in the lockers assigned to them. Tommy Joe was given the second bed in a line of 12 to 15 against the wall.

"Be good boys," said their aunt. "We must go now."

Tommy Joe and Lavern watched as the only people they knew in Georgia walked to their car and drove away. The reality of being orphans chilled them. The two things they had to be thankful for were the kindness of Rev. Buck and the fact that they had each other.

They were also used to being poor, so they quickly adjusted to conditions at Hephzibah. The boys at the Home each had two pairs of blue jeans—one pair to wear to school and one pair for chores. They went barefoot most of the time in warm weather.

Tommy Joe soon found out that life at Hephzibah was no picnic. The boys were wakened at 4:00 to go out to the barn and help milk the cows. Tommy Joe's eyes widened when he saw all those big cows. He watched as the other grabbed stools and pails and sat down beside the cows.

"Don'tcha' know how to milk?" called one.

Tommy Joe shook his head.

"City slicker, huh?" The boys laughed.

The name stuck. He was called "Slick" long after he learned to milk a cow! He learned a lot of other things, too—that cows had to be milked twice a day, that there were hogs and chickens to feed, fields to plow and sow and harvest, gardens to make, weeds to pull, butchering to be done. The Home depended on the farm operation for a lot of its income and food.

Tommy Joe's home when he arrived at Hephzibah

Tommy Joe Neyman (front row with arms outstretched)

Junior boys, May 8, 1949
Back row L to R: Gordon Lackey, Bailey Dodd, Steve Blanton, Bobby Ellis,
Dick Jones, Joe Neyman, Cullen Cooper, Ronald Maw.
Front row L to R: Albert Jones, Avery Jones, H. C. Lane, Lavern Neyman
with Carman Lane in front, Danny Dodd, Frank Jones, Vernon Lackey,
Jerry LeMay.

The girls had to work, too. They got up early to get the laundry done before they went to school. In late summer, truckloads of peaches were brought in and the girls worked in the hot kitchen peeling and canning them.

Sometimes the children got on the Hephzibah bus and went on an outing. The bus had the name of the Home in big letters on the sides. Tommy Joe hated the way people stared at the bus and at the children riding in it. When they got to their destination, they lined up outside the bus. The superintendent or one of the houseparents would give each child a little spending money.

That bothered Tommy Joe. They were not permitted to have money at the Home, even if they earned it. But sometimes the children hid their money. One time Tommy Joe had quite a little saved up and hidden away. But one of the other boys told on him. The superintendent asked him to bring his money to him. Joe did, but kept a little "nest egg" to build on!

Recreation was not a big feature at Hephzibah in those days. The children concocted their own games. Different kinds of ball were played. The boys played football barefooted!

One day the Hephzibah family attended a missionary service at the Wesleyan church in Macon. A man named A. J. (Archie) Argo was the speaker. Joe listened intently as Rev. Argo told of his work in Sierra Leone, West Africa. By this time Joe was established in his Christian life and had a deep desire to serve the Lord. While he was in this missionary service, God spoke to him, and Joe knew He was calling him to the mission field.

In high school, Tommy Joe was part of a group of boys at Hephzibah who were like brothers. They talked about what they would do when they left the Home, and hoped they could go to college together. Gordon Lackey and Dick Jones wanted to become teachers. Bill Maw and the others had their plans.

One day Joe learned that after he graduated from high school, the Hayworth Wesleyan Church in High Point, North Carolina, would have a place for him. They would help him find work and would help pay his college expenses.

High school graduation (1954) was coming up fast. Joe had a little trip planned. As a senior with good grades he was exempt from final exams and had a few days before the graduation exercises at Lanier High School in Macon. Taking $30 or $40 he had saved up, he packed the suitcase given to him for graduation and walked down to the highway (Forsyth Road) to hitchhike to Chattanooga. This visit to his sister there was the first he had made in five and a half years.

After graduating, he was ready to face the world on his own. The superintendent of the Home took him and another boy to Greenville,

South Carolina, where Joe caught a train for High Point. At first it seemed that he came as a surprise to the people at Hayworth. At least no definite plans were evident when he arrived.

Then two wonderful people came into Joe's life—Fred and Challie Ross. They took him into their home. What a mess he walked into that day! The Rosses were in the midst of painting their house, but they gave him a place to stay. This loving couple, who had no children of their own, gave Joe a key to their house.

"Our house is your house," they said. They were like parents to Joe and years later Joe's own children would call them Granddaddy and Grandma. The Rosses headed up the effort at Hayworth to raise Joe's college expenses. This was done through a "penny birthday offering."

Joe worked in a hosiery mill that summer and when fall came, he headed for Central Wesleyan College. There he joined up with the other boys from Hephzibah. His younger brother was there, too, to attend the academy. Everyone at Central College soon became aware of the "gang" from Hephzibah. This close-knit group gave evidence of the excellent training they had received. The students at the college, both boys and girls, looked up to the Hephzibah boys, who became famous for their games of "barefoot football" on the campus!

The college years were tough for Joe, who was never one to tell anyone about his personal needs. The Hayworth church had told him, "Let us know if you need anything." But Joe didn't feel free to do that. Without money to pay to get his clothes washed, he would wash them, including his blue jeans, by hand—sometimes without soap!

When he became part of the varsity quartet, he had the problem of a good suit to wear. Claude Rickman, the president, found out and let the Hayworth people know. A nice suit was soon forthcoming.

After graduating from college in 1958, Joe was offered a small pastorate in Graham, North Carolina. He wanted to go on to school at the University of North Carolina to prepare to be a missionary doctor. He decided he would do both—pastor and go to school. After going to his university classes all week, he drove to Graham on the weekend. It was a tiny church. When he took that pastorate he was told, "The church will have to go up because it can't go down any further!"

He found a little store building where he could stay at night. For his meals, he planned his calls to coincide with his parishioners' mealtimes. The little church was paying him $15 a week and sometimes he had to give part of that back to keep the lights on!

Since he never talked about his needs, no one in the church knew for quite some time that he was sleeping on the floor with no mattress and no heat. Finally, one of the members discovered his plight and found a cot and a heater for him.

One weekend a gospel team from Central College was scheduled to be at the Graham church. What did Joe think when he found out Shirley Stokes was on the team?

Dark-haired, tall and slender, Shirley finished nurse's training at Greenville, South Carolina. She was invited back to Central College to be school nurse while she took some more courses. Joe Neyman had dated her a few times and now she was coming with the gospel team.

Neither Joe nor Shirley will forget that special weekend. "That's when things began to get serious!" says Shirley.

After a year at the university, Joe decided to give full-time to the Graham church. He began bringing in children, some of whom, now grown, are on the church board. The church grew.

Joe and Shirley were married on June 4, 1960, by Rev. A. J. Argo, under whose ministry Joe had received his call. Together Joe and Shirley pastored the Graham church for two more years. During that time a baby boy was born, named Fred after Granddaddy Ross. The Neymans began planning toward going to the mission field. After applying to the missions department of The Wesleyan Methodist Church, they were accepted for service in Sierra Leone.

Shirley's heart was torn at this time, for her mother, in Rock Hill, South Carolina, was dying with cancer. Should they postpone their departure? Shirley talked with her mother, who loved missions and black people.

"Shirley, I'd rather die knowing you're on the mission field than have you stay here and nurse me."

Although bedridden, Mrs. Stokes felt the touch of God and was strengthened enough to go to the station to see Joe and Shirley and Freddy off on the train. One of Shirley's precious memories is the sight

*Joe and Shirley on their
wedding day*

*Fred and Darlynda
Neyman*

of her mother waving as the train pulled away. Shirley's eyes filled with tears. She knew she would not see her mother again in this world.

The Neymans arrived in Sierra Leone in June 1962 and were assigned to Kukuna. But for a month they were at Kamakwie while Dr. Wilbur Zike instructed Shirley in tropical medicine. Joe chafed a little under this, for he was left with Freddy and whatever language study he could get in. "Here I am in Africa and all I'm doing is baby-sitting!" he thought.

That quickly changed once they got to their station. Kukuna had been closed for four years. The Neymans settled in to work with the four existing churches and the dispensary. In 1964 a daughter, Darlynda, was born, the first missionary baby to be born in the Kamakwie Hospital.

In 1964 the Neymans had a year of furlough. Included in their travels was a trip to Hephzibah where a whole new campus greeted Joe.

When they returned to the field Shirley faced a hard thing. Of all that they had to give up to go to Africa, she didn't feel like she was sacrificing until they had to send Freddy many miles away to start first grade at Kabala.

The field at Kukuna seemed to be ripe. Joe loved getting new churches started—eight in all—so there were twelve by the time they finished their second term. He also helped build two new primary school buildings.

A curious thing began to happen while the Neymans were in Sierra Leone. Joe kept sensing a drawing toward Hephzibah. Was it just nostalgia for his old home? Was God trying to tell him something? This interest seemed to intensify during their second term. Joe needed to know if this was of the Lord.

Dr. V. A. Mitchell was scheduled to make an official visit to Sierra Leone and Joe began to pray, "Lord, if there's anything to it, if it's Your plan, then let Dr. Mitchell say something about it."

Dr. Mitchell came and on the last day of his stay, he said, "Joe, I want to talk to you." And he began talking about the situation at Hephzibah, where they had an interim superintendent.

"If you're interested," said Dr. Mitchell, "contact Dr. B. H. Phaup, who is the chairman of the Hephzibah board."

Joe wrote to Dr. Phaup, who responded that the door was closed! That was that, thought Joe, and went on with preparations to furlough that summer (1969). Upon their return to the United States, the Neymans went first to High Point where some of their things were stored, reaching there on Saturday. The next day after service at Hayworth, one of Joe's friends came up to him. "Congratulations!" he said.

"For what?"

"Didn't you know you've been appointed superintendent at Hephzibah?"

When they got to Shirley's father's place, they found a letter waiting with confirmation. The interim superintendent, Rev. M. L. Arnold, stayed on until the Neymans had fulfilled their obligations to the missions department.

The Neyman family moved to Macon in December of 1969, and a new era began for Hephzibah Children's Home.

Chapter 14

The Neyman Years

When Joe and Shirley Neyman, nine-year-old Freddy and five-year-old Darlynda moved into the superintendent's house at Hephzibah, it must have seemed a little like coming home—at least to Joe. But the campus had been transformed. No more iron beds in a big room, no more milking cows twice a day, no more slipping through red mud, no more playing in the woods.

The farm operation had been discontinued in 1959, the same year the Home property had been annexed to the city of Macon. Two years before Joe became superintendent, almost 41 acres had been sold to a realtor, leaving 16.5 acres for the campus. The pecan grove was still down on the front lawn, the trees a little bigger now.

But the main thing that hadn't changed was the children, and that was why Joe was there. No other superintendent had ever looked at those children quite like Joe did. He thought of himself, not as a boss or a father, but as a brother, who sat where they sat and walked where they walked." He knew the security that came when provision was made, not only for food, clothing and shelter, but for consistent discipline, religious instruction, recreation and Christian role models.

When the Home got a new bus, Joe said, "No name on the sides. I know what it's like to be stared at when you're on a bus from a children's home!" He also began giving the children an allowance. Not

Joe and Shirley Neyman

Leonard Teel as a child

Hephzibah children in 1974

only did they need to be trusted, they needed to learn how to manage money.

One of Mr. Neyman's gifts was dealing with children lovingly but firmly. His friendliness, his teasing, his time spent with them, his sensitivity to their needs—these provided a firm foundation for his relationships with the boys and girls. Then when discipline was needed, even though it may have seemed harsh, they accepted it because of the love that was behind it.

Leo's story illustrates this relationship. His home was all too typical for Hephzibah children. His father was an alcoholic and his mother didn't seem to want to bother with the six children. Leo and three of his sisters went to Hephzibah when he was about ten years old. After the chaos of his family, Leo found the security in the junior boys' cottage quite comforting.

But Leo had some problems. He was behind his grade level in school. Miss Geraldine Fortune, his housemother for awhile, spent hours tutoring him. With diligent effort his schoolwork improved. But it wasn't smooth sailing, for Leo couldn't hold still for long and his actions were unpredictable.

The boys in Miss Fortune's cottage chafed under her strict attention to cleanliness. Beds were to be made just so, and not a speck of dust was to be found. (Leo says Miss Fortune made his basic training in the Air Force a lot easier!)

On one occasion when even the patient Miss Fortune decided a paddling was in order, Leo got upset and told her, "Well, if there's a heaven and you're going there, I don't want to go!" Yet years after leaving Hephzibah, Leo admits, "I can never repay all Miss Fortune has done for me."

It was hard to hold still for the devotions in the dining hall every morning, but Leo began to look forward to Mr. Neyman's Bible stories. That Bible knowledge was stored up in Leo's mind and he treasures it today.

Another problem Leo had was yielding to the temptation to steal. The staff thought he was stealing to get attention, but Leo says he stole to get things he wanted! Time after time Mr. Neyman took Leo into his office and spanked him when he was caught stealing. But spankings had no effect on Leo.

One day Leo was caught stealing something in a convenience store, and he soon found himself facing Mr. Neyman in his office. Leo tried to lie his way out of it, but he knew Mr. Neyman saw right through that—yes, right through Leo's soul. The superintendent's gaze pierced the boy's heart. Then Mr. Neyman dropped his head and said, "Get out of my office!"

Leo slowly walked out, a strange feeling clutching his heart. He's given up on me! He thought. The person I love most in the world doesn't know what to do with me. Something happened to Leo that day and the stealing stopped.

In the dining hall one mealtime Leo and his friend, Randall, sat at the same table with Mr. Neyman. Dessert was banana pudding. While Mr. Neyman was away from the table, Randall cast covetous eyes on the superintendent's dish of pudding. When he returned, he pulled his dessert toward him, ready to enjoy the treat.

"I want it!" Randall grabbed at it playfully.

"Here—you eat it." Mr. Neyman pushed it toward him.

This small incident stuck in Leo's mind. To him, it represented many sacrifices this man made for the Hephzibah family.

The children appreciated Mr. Neyman's humor and teasing. Sometimes he "put one over" on the adults, too.

Through the years Hephzibah has often been able to fill their big freezer with meat through donations. Sometimes the highway patrolmen brought in deer that had been hit by a car. One time they brought in a bear, which Joe butchered.

When it was Hephzibah's turn to host the meeting for workers in the city's children homes, case- and court-workers, two large platters of meat were on the table. One was ham and one was steaks. The guests kept eating the steaks. After the meal was over, Joe told them those were bear steaks.

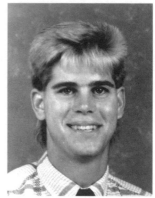

Bart Neyman

"You'll never get me to eat any of that bear!" declared Dorothy Allison.

Some time later, hamburgers were on the dining hall menu. Since this was not Dorothy's favorite, she usually took only one. But they were so delicious that day that she ate two. After supper Joe asked her, "How did you like the bearburgers?"

Shirley Neyman worked with her husband, often in unseen ways, to make Hephzibah the success that it is. Her influence was felt in many areas. On staff as a nurse and a case worker, she was called upon for innumerable other responsibilities.

One of her special labors of love began as the Christmas season approached. Churches and individuals began to write in to ask for gift suggestions. Shirley responded to these many requests, sending sizes for clothing and itemizing needs.

The clothing room in the pole barn was prepared as the "Santa Claus Room." Windows were covered, and the mysterious packages began to arrive. As the flow of UPS deliveries increased, the truck driver bypassed the main office and drove right up to the Santa Claus Room. Sorting and coordinating gifts for 30 to 40 children (besides staff) was a time-consuming task. In some cases, money was sent and Shirley went shopping for the needed items. Houseparents and others helped wrap the gifts, and finally Hephzibah was ready for another exciting Christmas. Shirley also made sure that letters were sent to all donors thanking them for their gifts.

Children at Hephzibah ordinarily are not up for adoption. Bart was an exception, and his story turned out to be unique.

When he was admitted to the junior boys' cottage at age 11, Bart was confused, hurt, and nearing despair. Taken from his natural family, he had been adopted by a couple in Macon. It was a disastrous decision, for he did not become a real part of his new family. His life was miserable and he ran away several times.

104

Finally the parents had had enough and they turned Bart over to the welfare department. "He is no longer part of our family!" they said. Bart's caseworker arranged for him to be admitted to Hephzibah. He proved to be quite a challenge for the staff, for he had picked up the habits of smoking "pot" and of shoplifting.

When Bart was 12 years old the welfare agency decided that they were going to see that he was adopted again. By this time he was in the senior boys' cottage. Arrangements were made for him to go to Atlanta and appear on the television show "Wednesday's Child" where children available for adoption were interviewed. Following the program on which Bart appeared, 60 people made contact with an interest in adopting Bart.

But God had other plans. One day Shirley Neyman was washing dishes and looked out the kitchen window to see Bart walking up from the senior boys' cottage. At that moment God spoke to her, "I want you and Joe to adopt Bart."

Overwhelmed by surprise, she ran from the kitchen and said to her daughter, Darlynda, "Guess what! I feel God wants us to adopt Bart!" When she told her husband, he said, "Well, don't say anything to anyone until we see." But he was in favor of the idea.

One day Bart was sitting at the table in Neymans' kitchen talking with Darlynda. He listened carefully as she told him how Jesus wanted to be his Savior. His heart was open and that was the day he became a Christian. He has grown steadily stronger in the faith since that time.

When the Neymans went on summer vacation for two weeks, Bart spent one week with them. The next step was to make their desire known to the caseworker at the Department of Family and Children's Services. When the caseworker heard Shirley's statement about wanting to adopt Bart, she looked at her in amazement, saying, "Oh, Mrs. Neyman, you will never know what an answer to prayer you are!"

"Why?" Shirley asked.

"Because Bart had told me he does not want to leave Hephzibah."

The Neymans felt God was moving. Bart warmed to the idea of being part of their family. The adoption was finalized when Bart was 13 years old. One month after that, they discovered Bart was a diabetic. His adoptive mother (Shirley Neyman) had the same problem and he had always said, "I hope I'm never a diabetic!"

Being with a family that already coped with this disease made it easier for Bart. He takes insulin twice a day but doesn't let his physical lack slow him down. After high school graduation he went to Central Wesleyan College to major in business and to play soccer. His sensitivity to others, his loving disposition, his many capabilities—all have brought much joy to the entire Neyman family.

Although a gymnasium, a "pole barn" and other additions were made to the campus during Mr. Neyman's administration, the lasting, priceless building was done in the lives of the children.

In June 1982 *Hephzibah's Happenings* carried a letter to the *Macon Telegraph and News* for a Father's Day contest, written by Lynn Hudson, a young lady in the Home.

I would like to tell you about a man that I love very much. As far as men go, he is of average height and weight. Over the years he has gotten a little thinner on top, but his lack of hair is his only deficiency. He is a man of God and practices what he preaches. Even though we have a large family, he somehow makes time for each child. Besides his many weekly duties, he also teaches a Sunday school class at Bel Arbor Nursing Home.

Just like any other family, our family had many needs and occasional problems, all of which fall upon the shoulders of Rev. Joe Neyman. Most of the children fondly refer to Rev. Neyman as Papa Joe rather than Daddy. Papa Joe makes sure all of us have nice clothes to wear and plenty of good food to eat. Every Sunday he delivers a message designed to help us in our daily lives. He desires only the best for us and encourages us to make the most of every opportunity in order that we might become productive members of society. He is always there when we need him, whether it be to discuss a problem, show him a good report card, or try to talk him out of a spanking.

Rev. Joe Neyman truly exemplifies the name 'Dad.' Even though he is not my dad in a legal sense, he is in every other way. Rev. Neyman is the superintendent of Hephzibah Children's Home. Mr. Neyman is a very concerned man who knows very well that he cannot replace our fathers; however he does an excellent job of filling the void that came about as a result of this loss.

Mr. Neyman served Hephzibah Children's Home as superintendent (now General Director) from 1969 until June of 1992, at which time he resigned and accepted a Georgia pastorate. The trust of his district was evidenced by his simultaneous service on the Georgia District Board of Administration and on the District Camp Board.

Every superintendent of the Home tries to put together a staff of "team players." A director is blessed when he latches onto a worker with staying power. Not all those who feel drawn to the Home have this quality. In fact, one lady who came to be a houseparent stayed only one night. Another was there for a few days, but one night she locked herself into her room and refused to come out. She was through!

Since the Hephzibah chronicle is a story about people, this account mandates at least a mention of the following who served with distinction during the Neyman years.

Geraldine Fortune

The little white house had been a chicken house, a garage, a shoe repair shop, and a guest house. Later bricked, it became home to two ladies who were part of the "Neyman team." One of the ladies in the little house was Geraldine Fortune, a graduate of Central Wesleyan College. She was in her second year of teaching first grade in South Carolina when a former pastor told her there was a need for houseparents at Hephzibah. "Maybe you'd be interested and would like to pray about it," he said.

"All right." But there wasn't much interest on her part. Still, the idea had been planted, and it kept surfacing. So she decided she should think and pray about it. Finally she said to the Lord, "I will go to Hephzibah for a year. If I like it, I will stay longer."

The Lord did not give her joy over this decision. Peace came only when she said, "Lord, I'll go and stay as long as You want me to!"

When her mother heard about her decision, she wasn't exactly enthusiastic. Mrs. Fortune had visited the Home before Geraldine was born and had described it to her. Geraldine told the Lord it was hard to go when her mother was not happy about it. Geraldine was her youngest daughter and she was reluctant for her to leave home. God gave Geraldine Mark 10:29-30 as her assurance, and she knew that no matter what she gave up for Jesus' sake—father or mother or lands—He would abundantly reward her. Her mother became very supportive once Geraldine got to Hephzibah.

Geraldine sensed that God used her mother's reluctance to help her know that He was leading her. It was not something someone else told

Geraldine Fortune

her to do. After she got to the Home and worked as junior girls' houseparent, she knew why God had taken pains to make her call definite. Otherwise she would have left in two weeks!

Like all other Hephzibah staff, she really didn't know what she was getting into until she got there. She was so eager to go that she went to her first-grade room the last day of school and gave out report cards, then drove to Macon the same day—without taking any vacation. Upon arrival this 25-

year-old became an "instant" mother of twelve girls, ages six to fourteen! Could this slender, soft-spoken woman handle it?

The junior girls had not had a houseparent for some time. Here was their chance to "try out" this young "mother." But Geraldine made up her mind she was going to stay and when the girls accepted that, things settled down. Then she could begin to give them the security they so desperately needed.

The first year at the Home, she received $98 a month as salary. Her car payment was $72, life insurance $9, and after tithe and gas, she had less than one dollar left. Then she got a bill for her city and county taxes for $24.90. She told no one but her Heavenly Father. Then she received a $5 Christmas bonus from the Home. And just before the taxes were due she got an anonymous Christmas card, mailed from Macon, with $20 in it.

After four years as junior girls' houseparent, Miss Fortune went back to teaching and was away from Hephzibah for three years. During that time she had surgery. When she returned to the Home in 1970 she became part of Joe Neyman's team. A draining half year as relief houseparent and she switched jobs with the office secretary. After a time she became Mr. Neyman's assistant and was in charge when he was off campus.

Following the resignation of Joe Neyman as General Director, Geraldine Fortune was appointed Interim Director on July 27, 1992, with a request that she serve during the search and election process. Although Geraldine declined to let her name stand as a nominee for the office, she served with excellence until the Board of Directors named a new director on January 30, 1993. After 27 years of devoted service to Hephzibah Children's Home, Geraldine resigned from the staff on June 23, 1993, and joined the staff at Southern Wesleyan University. On February 25, 1995, she became the bride of C. B. Masters and devoted herself to the joys of being a full-time homemaker.

Frances Good

The other occupant of the little brick house was Frances Good. Unlike most of the other workers, Frances came from a background similar to that of many of the children at the Home. Her father was an alcoholic who worked on the railroad. His wife and family of twelve eked out a living in Albany, New York. The Good family moved to the country and at the pastor's invitation, seven or eight of the children began attending the Watervliet Wesleyan Methodist Church.

Rev. Kenneth Ross came as pastor at Watervliet when Frances was in the tenth grade. She knew she didn't want to live the kind of life her parents lived, and she gave her life to Christ. Her mother changed her mind about the children attending, tore up the Sunday school books and forbade them to go. Frances quit school, got a job

Frances Good

and went out on her own so she could keep on going to church.

After two years the Rosses asked her to move in with them and provided a Christian home for her until she was 26. She moved with them when they went to pastor in West Chazy. They suggested she might like to work at Hephzibah. She hadn't graduated from high school, so she was doubtful they would hire her. But she sent a letter of inquiry, and after some phone calls, it was settled.

In May 1962 Frances Good packed three suitcases, and the Rosses took her to the bus. She cried when she saw them walk away. Her first weekend at Hephzibah she was relief houseparent for 12 junior boys. She almost panicked. What did she know about the rules or the routine? And here was a mountain of laundry to do. Tackling it as best she could, she loaded the washer with blue jeans and poured in soap—and bleach. When the housemother came back on duty, she was horrified to find a pile of ruined jeans. In her frustration she scolded Frances.

"I cried and cried," she recalls. "I was going back home—but I'm still here!"

Leaving the Home in 1965, she worked at other jobs, spent some time in the hospital, went to night school, and did volunteer work. Learning that Dorothy Allison was ready to take a vacation, Frances offered to take care of her girls.

In 1973 Joe Neyman asked Frances if she'd like to come back and work at the Home. "Where would you like to work?" he asked.

Workers' cottage where Miss Fortune and Miss Good lived

"Relief houseparent!"

"You're crazy!" He laughed, but took her at her word and hired her as relief houseparent. She stuck it out for many years—15 years of living out of a suitcase. Onto a little wire two-wheeled cart she would pile her bedroll and her bag and stay at each of the four cottages one night a week while the houseparent took their night off, in turn. Then Frances spent the weekend at the cottage where the houseparents had the weekend off (every fifth weekend).

One time the children put a frog in the drawer of the room where she would be staying. Ever since then she's been called Miss Froggy. She now has a frog collection to match Mr. Towner's goats!

The job Frances had that she liked best was mailing out the quarterly newsletter *Hephzibah Happenings*. When she took it over in 1975 there were 3500 on the mailing list. By 1980 there were 30,000. It took three weeks to get them all mailed. Frances put stacks of the newsletters on her little cart and worked on putting on labels wherever she was.

Mike and Jan Manley

Mike and Jan Manley were members of the Neyman team. In 1979, they had been accepted as missionaries for The Wesleyan Church to Indonesia and had taken their missionary internship. They had begun to break their ties with the Community Wesleyan Church where they had been pastoring in Columbia, Mississippi, thinking they would be going to Indonesia at the end of the district year.

Then in late 1979 came the distressing report on Tod, one of their infant twin boys—he had cerebral palsy. Their missionary career ended before it even began. Soon after, they received a newsletter from Hephzibah—the first one they remembered seeing. It carried the appeal for someone to come as houseparents for senior boys.

After a visit to the Home and much prayer, the Manleys moved to Macon. Jan's job was senior boys' houseparent, while Mike was director of development—and houseparent at night! Twins Jon and Tod were 16 months old when they became part of the Hephzibah family, and Jan had three senior boys.

Things went well for several months. Then a new senior boy named Ken* arrived—right at mealtime, and decided he didn't even want to get out of the car. Then that night he didn't want to take a shower. But Mike and Jan kept firmly insisting.

Mike and Jan Manley with Jon (standing) and Tod

*Not real name

110

Taking Ken to church the first time was an unsettling experience. He kept acting like he was going to get up. Sitting beside him, Jan kept her hand on his arm and gave a firm squeeze every time he moved!

Soon after Ken came, the senior boys increased from four to eight in one day! Later the number of boys increased to nine. Mike needed to be free to travel, but he felt hesitant to leave Jan to care for Jon and Tod and nine teenagers by herself, a job that was becoming increasingly difficult. They felt that God was directing them to make a change, and so after one year and eight months of houseparenting, they bought a house off campus. Jan worked as a pediatric nurse practitioner in the city health department while Mike continued in public relations.

The 1984-85 year was spent at another children's home in Texas. But Mike admits there wasn't a day that he didn't think about Hephzibah. So they moved back to Macon and Mike picked up where he left off, traveling across the denomination to present the Home to the Church. This tall, black-haired "ambassador" for Hephzibah became a familiar figure across the denomination. Jan was hired as caseworker and nurse.

Hephzibah is required to have at least a consultant who has a master's degree in social work. At that time they had someone off campus who theoretically was available but wasn't actually as involved as the situation required. In the fall of 1985 Jan had an opportunity to begin work on a master's degree in social work by going to classes at an extension setup from the University of Georgia. She finished in June 1988 and brought to Hephzibah the much-needed, on-site, qualified social worker.

Ruby Hudson

Within weeks after Manleys got to Hephzibah, another team member arrived. Raised a Southern Baptist, Ruby Hudson went back to college after her divorce and became a certified teacher for kindergarten through ninth grade. While she was teaching in Gastonia, North Carolina, she began attending the Firestone Wesleyan Church. A year later she was elected YMWB director and that was when she first heard about Hephzibah.

Feeling the Lord was nudging her in that direction, she told her parents she was thinking about going there. But Ruby had two daughters to care for, and she wouldn't want to go until after the older one, Lynn, graduated from high school. She decided to send to Hephzibah for an application, even though Lynn had two more years. When the application came, she laid it aside.

A year went by. In the summer of 1980, Ruby was working at the beach in "Sand and Surf"—vacation Bible school. While she was there the Lord told her it was time to send in that application to Hephzibah.

Ruby Hudson

What? Lynn still had another year of school, she thought. Ruby had already signed a teaching contract and gotten her classroom ready for fall.

Obedient to God's leading, she sent the application in at the end of July and quickly got a phone call from Joe Neyman asking her to come for a visit. It was nothing like she expected. She thought there would be little wood houses!

Joe wanted her to come right away. The senior girls' cottage had not had a houseparent since Dorothy Allison left in 1978. Ruby prayed that God would show Lynn that this was His will. A smooth transition was made. Ruby moved into the senior girls' cottage with her daughters, Lynn and Susan, and three senior girls. As time passed, other girls came, and Ruby sometimes had up to ten in her group during her seven and one-half years as houseparent.

Lynn had a wonderful senior year in a Macon high school before going to college. Susan was left to take the brunt of being the houseparent's child. Some of the girls would get mad at Ruby and take it out on Susan.

Ruby is a jolly, creative person who brought a needed dimension to the Hephzibah team.

Eileen Burris

All summer the staff looked forward to the day in the fall when Eileen Burris would return to Hephzibah. After spending the summer at her home in Lapel, Indiana, Eileen drove to Macon where she worked at the Home for eight or nine months.

Soon after her husband died in 1968, the Wesleyan church in Fisherburg where she attended was packing a box to send to Hephzibah. She put some things in it. That was the first she had heard of the home.

Due to retire after thirty years at General Motors, Eileen began to think of what she could do to keep busy. She decided she would visit Hephzibah for a few days in July 1977. That was a memorable visit. With the temperature at 105 degrees, she stopped at a phone booth when she got to Macon and called the Home for directions to get there. The person who answered put her on hold and went to get someone who could tell her how to get to the Home from where she was. Minutes seemed like hours in the stifling heat.

Arriving finally, with a headache, she was horrified to discover that Hephzibah had no air conditioning. She was about ready to turn around and go back to Indiana. But Joe Neyman interviewed her for an hour.

"Can you type? Can you? . . ." And he named several things to which Eileen kept saying, "No."

"All I can do is sew and cook," she told him.

"Well, come on," he said. And she's been coming ever since.

Eileen Burris

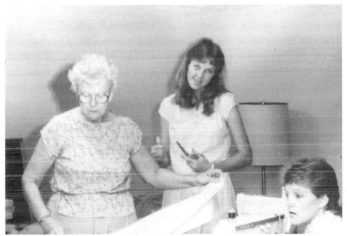

Eileen Burris with Diamond Chamberlin (standing) and Angie Fields (1985)

Eileen went as a worker in January 1979. For two years she stayed in the senior girls' cottage (not as a houseparent) and did mending and sewed clothes for them. Through the years she has helped in the kitchen, done grocery buying, helped with the paperwork of the government food program, and done a lot of errands, using her car to take children and staff here and there.

One of her memorable accomplishments was to make the dresses the Hephzibah girls wore when they sang at the Knoxville General Conference.

No longer does Eileen stay on campus but has her own apartment downtown. All her work is donated.

Joan Edwards

Many members of the Neyman team have come and gone. Among these is Joan Edwards. A missionary in Puerto Rico for several years, Joan brought many talents to her work at Hephzibah. Serving as houseparent for awhile, she then became secretary, which was something she did especially well. Her writing ability served the Home admirably when she wrote articles about Hephzibah for *The Young Missionary* (YMWB publication). Her tenure at the Home was from 1979 to 1986. Her mother, "Granny" Edwards, also contributed time and effort to service at Hephzibah.

Houseparents

In the fall of 1988 houseparents at Hephzibah were Warren and Esther Bennett (senior girls), Frank and Thelma McCool (senior boys), Howell and Myrtle Kifer (junior girls) and Tom and Linda Miller (junior boys). Volumes could be written detailing experiences of houseparents. Shared here is a memory capsule from Tom and Linda Miller.

Jeremy hurried into the utility room, pulled the vacuum cleaner from the storage area, plugged it in, flipped the switch and began cleaning the square of carpet by the back door. Just turned six, Jeremy was the youngest of the junior boys. He and his brother had come to Hephzibah a few months earlier and Jeremy was surprised when his face appeared on the full color Hephzibah poster.

The junior boys had just come from the dining hall in another building and had about half an hour to clean their cottage before going to school. This was the morning to wet-mop the floors. Tom Miller, houseparent, was the sergeant leading the troops. But he also worked *with* them. Besides straightening their rooms, the boys had other assigned chores.

Each bedroom, the hall, entry, living room, kitchen, activity room and study room had to be dry-mopped. Furniture was moved in the living area and the wet-mopping followed quickly. The boys sat on the displaced couches and chairs while the floors dried. Then the buffing process began.

Time was running short as the boys finished their work, hurried to the utility room where Linda Miller was folding the laundry. In between chores the boys had been taking their clean clothes from the shelf and the hooks, each marked by initials, and putting them in their rooms. Heading out the back door each boy reached for his books and papers in another cubbyhole marked by his name.

"Bye, Jeremy! Don't forget your library book!" called Linda. "Your hair looks nice, Tony. Have a good day!"

Suddenly quiet reigned. The Millers had a rare moment together

114

Tom and Linda Miller

before heading for other tasks. He had a computer class and a driver's education class, plus a new computer system he was to learn and program for the Home. She had the ever-present laundry besides baby-sitting for some of the small children of the academy teachers.

"It went OK this morning." Tom grinned at his wife, who smiled back. They were remembering the many times it didn't go OK. How could they forget those awful weeks and months when they were new houseparents?

The Millers attended the Bethany Wesleyan Church in Cherryville, Pennsylvania, and were involved in bus ministry and children's church. For some time they had sensed that God had something special for them to do for Him. In the summer of 1984, a friend began talking with them about the possibility of her going to Hephzibah as a houseparent. Through these discussions they kept getting input about the Home. Then a missionary speaker in July presented a message titled "Are You Willing to Pay the Price?" In August came another missionary who said he had never expected to be a missionary but God started opening the doors.

A November issue of *The Wesleyan Advocate* carried an appeal for houseparents at Hephzibah. The Millers decided to send for information. In a week they received applications and Tom sent his in.

Weeks passed and they heard nothing. They found out later that Joe and Shirley Neyman, the director and his wife, were so busy filling in as houseparents that they didn't have time to respond. At last arrangements were made. Joe was to visit them in their home. "But I have only one application," he said over the phone. "I need one from Linda."

But Linda put if off. It wasn't until Joe got to their house that she finished filling out the application in the bedroom while Tom entertained Joe in the living room. They had questions galore. Then in February they visited Hephzibah for two days.

"What are you looking for in houseparents?" they asked Joe.

"Basically, three things: flexibility, good common sense and few 'hang-ups.' You have to be able to work with the kids where they are without 'labeling' them."

The need at Hephzibah drew them. Their ministries at Cherryville seemed to have prepared them for being houseparents. But if the Lord had showed them then what they were getting into, they would have said, "No way!"

Into a U-Haul trailer went their clothes and some personal items and the Millers headed south. They arrived at Hephzibah March 11, 1985, Tom's 39th birthday. They were on duty as soon as they moved into the junior boys' cottage.

Like any missionary, they experienced culture shock. Barriers confronted them. As Northerners they learned that some people were still "fighting the Civil War!" The change in climate meant another adjustment. But the highest, thickest barrier of all was one put up by the boys.

The honeymoon—when the boys knew nothing about them and they knew nothing about the boys—was short-lived. Then began a refrain that lasted for 18 months.

"The other houseparents didn't do it that way."

"We did this or that when they were here."

Before 1985 the junior boys' cottage had a high rate of turnover of houseparents. Soon after arriving, the Millers heard the boys saying, "We're going to run off the Millers just like we did the other houseparents!"

Tom and Linda tried to take it one day at a time, insisting, "This is the way the Millers are going to do it." But it was tough going and the opposition was strong. The boys didn't want to accept their new houseparents.

A chink opened in the wall through one of the senior boys named Jimmy Sivic, an athletic fellow who loved sports—as did Tom Miller.

"Come on, Jimmy, I'll hit you fly balls," Tom said one day. All afternoon Tom played ball with Jimmy, both obviously having a great time, while the junior boys looked on. Jimmy helped Tom get his foot in the door and slowly the boys came around. And as they began to play together, they began to work together.

Chore time was the war zone. After breakfast the boys flocked to the bathroom to brush their teeth—a perfect excuse for elbowing each other. Then, with belligerent reluctance they turned to the chores.

"Why do we have to mop the floors?" they asked repeatedly.

"Because I like to live in a clean house," was Tom's reply. Then he plunged in and worked with them.

The hostility and suspicion persisted. Perversely, the boys would show affection to the houseparents of the junior girls and talk about how mean the Millers were. Tom and Linda intervened in quarrels and fights, only to have the boys turn on *them*. Minutes later the two fighters were the best of buddies while the Millers were still churning inside.

"What are we doing wrong?" they wondered. At rare intervals they got the chance to talk with other houseparents and were surprised and sadly relieved to discover that they were having the same problems.

116

Gradually they became aware of the system within the system. The kids had their own goals and ran their own system while the Millers tried to run theirs. The kids' strategy was to make the houseparents feel guilty. "How'd you ever get to be a houseparent? You don't know what you're talking about!" They were experts at making the adults feel like they were the problem—not the kids!

Part of the system was the "games" the boys played. One, already described, was "let's you and him fight." This tactic guaranteed an upset houseparent. It took time to settle the quarrel, get the facts, talk it through. It didn't help to realize later that the quarrel was for the most part a diversionary maneuver.

Military terms are apt, for a battle was going on. Linda poured out her soul in a diary for the first 18 months. Periodically interspersed in the woes and frustrations was the phrase, "When the battle's over we shall wear a crown." She and Tom clung to "their" verse in Psalms: "If thy law had not been my delight then I would have perished in my affliction."

One day off per week just didn't come often enough or last long enough. They went to a motel and tried to sleep off six days of exhaustion. Only every fifth week did they get a weekend off.

Tom and Linda, after 18 months, finally got control of the cottage. It took that long for all the boys, who were there when they came, to return to their homes or to move on to the senior boys' cottage. Then they had a group that was "theirs." The Millers were the only houseparents they had known, and now they could really build security in these children's lives.

Randall Ballard

Responsibility of the Home to a child terminated either when he/she went back to parents or ended schooling. If a child quit school at 16 he/she had to leave the Home. Many finished high school. If they went on to college, they were still part of the Hephzibah family until graduation. But no program was provided for those who leave after high school. Some married, some got jobs, but some did neither. The adjustments of young people in our Wesleyan families at this stage of life remind us of the rocky road they travel. How much harder for teens who have no home backing.

Randall Ballard's story illustrates the problem. Born February 14, 1960, in Gastonia, North Carolina, Randall was

Randall Ballard

117

the oldest of six children. The father was never at home and the family was eventually separated and placed by twos with family and friends. Randall's grandmother was a member of the Wesleyan church in Charlotte, North Carolina.

Then Randall's mother, who felt utterly inadequate to cope with all her problems, attempted suicide. This prompted action to get the children into the stable environment provided at Hephzibah. The Ballard children arrived sometime in 1970, and Randall began receiving the acceptance, love and security he needed.

The six years at the Home were beautiful for Randall. The love of the Neymans, of Miss Fortune and Miss Good and others meant a great deal to the confused young redhead.

By the time Randall was 16, his parents had divorced and married other partners. He was sent to live with his father and stepmother, but the adjustment was too great for all concerned. Randall went out on his own, worked long hours in a furniture factory for $2.40 an hour, and at the same time, finished high school.

After two years of "all work and no play" Randall began running with the wrong crowd and started going from job to job. The six years after leaving Hephzibah were as miserable as the previous six years had been happy. Knocking around over Georgia and North Carolina, Randall sensed God had not forgotten him. He heard God tell him to get away from his friends, and in the summer of 1982 he ended up in Macon, where he got a job the next day.

In October of that year Randall gave his heart to the Lord at a Hephzibah church service. Within two months God had opened the door for him to attend Bartlesville Wesleyan College.

Graduating in May 1987 with a bachelor's degree in behavioral science and an emphasis in Christian counseling, Randall felt he would some day be in pastoral ministries. It would take only a few hours more of college.

Three small buildings (L to R): Sugar shack (storage building); classroom K-3; three rooms (classroom, principal's office, pastor's office)

118

Gymnasium

Pole barn (science classroom on left, clothing room on right, swimming pool in background)

Hephzibah Academy

After working in a Tulsa, Oklahoma, boys' home for a time, he became assistant director of a halfway house, a treatment center, with The Salvation Army. Then the program was discontinued after seven or eight months and Randall was back on the streets, looking for work. Two months of this exhausted his savings and he decided to head for home—Hephzibah. Arriving there in the fall of 1988, he stepped into the job of houseparent at the junior boys' cottage.

"I'd always wanted to work at Hephzibah," he says, and the Lord had prepared him for it.

Because of God's grace, Randall provided to these boys the love and patience that made a difference in his life.

Like Randall, many of the youth who leave Hephzibah in their late teens face a struggle. Often their families, if they have a family, feel they are old enough to be on their own and cannot afford to help them. A high school graduate can rarely get a job that pays enough to provide an apartment, a car and other necessities.

Accordingly, it was a glad day when occupancy of the new campus in 1997 provided facilities designed for a transitional living program. Although this account appropriately belongs in a subsequent chapter, it is here noted that the new Hephzibah campus provides a place for residents ages 18-25 to receive their basic housing, food and clothing needs, along with limited supervision. This arrangement assists them in becoming self-sufficient in living skills, education and employment.

Campus School and Church

Hephzibah has had a long and checkered history in its relationships with public schools. In the early years the children were taught in the orphanage. Under the Wesleyans this was discontinued. No matter how clean and nicely dressed the children were, they could not escape being called Hephzibah kids.

As there were more children from problem homes and fewer orphans, the problems increased. Typically, the children came from homes where parents took little interest in the education of their offspring. They were too absorbed with their drinking, marital problems, and unemployment to bother with homework or even getting the children to school. A child from this background probably had moved many times each year. Inevitably, he would be two or three grades below the level he should be.

When these children came to Hephzibah and then went to the public schools, it became the responsibility of houseparents to try to see that homework was done. How do you plan your evening to help eight or ten children in several different grades?

The Home staff knew that these children soon made friends with the group in the schools that had the same kind of home background they did.

Carolyn Gay

Darlynda Neyman

There was little incentive or encouragement from their peers toward self-improvement. In fact, some of the children spent so much time in detention that they got farther and farther behind. At times, it tended to become a "badge of courage" to be the one from Hephzibah who got expelled from school that day. One or two of the children did anything to keep from having to go to school—induce vomiting or cause a nosebleed. Or if they did get to school, they might never get inside it. One boy spent the first day of school in the woods. He came out with a grand case of poison ivy!

Faced with problems like these, it is no wonder that the Hephzibah staff began dreaming of having their own school. Years of hoping, wishing and praying preceded the board's decision—at last—to start planning for a school. The advantages would be great: smaller student/teacher ratio, less peer pressure, tailor-made instruction, and closer cooperation between teachers and houseparents.

Detractors said the children were going to be too sheltered, that they needed to be out in the community. But the Hephzibah staff knew the children too well. These kids had already seen the world. They needed a little sheltering!

Fred and Ruth Neyman and Sara

Geraldine Fortune and Ruby Hudson worked with Mr. Neyman and others to plan for the school. They visited other private schools, examined curricula, met with public school officials, tried to find teachers, drew up a budget, considered a thousand and one details, and prayed!

Ruby Hudson, often wondering why God brought her

to Hephzibah to be a houseparent when she was trained as a teacher, had experience, and dearly loved it, was excited about getting the school started. Another helpful person was Mrs. Carolyn Gay. Since about 1976 she had tutored Hephzibah children after school under Chapter 1 (a federal grant program). Her specialty was reading and she was ready to become a part of the Hephzibah Academy when it opened. God provided trained teachers for this fledgling educational venture.

Classrooms needed to be prepared, and the children were asked to help. But they had not been told about the school! When they helped prepare two rooms down in the gym, they thought they must be Sunday school rooms. The school operated in seven classrooms on the campus. When the second semester of the 1983-84 school year was about to begin, Mr. Neyman told the children that they would not be going to public school the next day but would stay at the Home. The children's faces registered utter amazement.

Miss Fortune was the school's first principal. Then the job was turned over to Ruth Neyman, wife of Fred Neyman. Daughter of Rev. and Mrs. Kenneth Gorveatte, Ruth is a Canadian citizen and mother of Sara, born November 15, 1985. Fred and Ruth were married in May 1982 and spent that summer traveling in behalf of Hephzibah. In the fall they returned to Central College for Fred's senior year. After Ruth's resignation as principal in 1992, Mrs. Elsie Daniels accepted appointment and led the school during the next two years.

The eleven years in which the school operated brought rewarding results. The children gained a better self-image. More of the high school students finished instead of dropping out in their junior year. The "unknown" factors of public school teachers and students were eliminated. Needs were identified and met more easily, with closer cooperation between school and the cottages. The ABEKA curriculum was used, and the first class every day was a Bible class.

Isolation was prevented in part by getting the children involved in various community activities, such as Little League. Some older children had part-time jobs.

The children not only went to school on the Hephzibah campus, they and the staff attended church at the Home. Services at the Home were routine in the early years and continued until a Wesleyan church began in Macon in 1947. The story has been recounted in an earlier chapter.

The brick church on Morgan Street in Macon, called Tyler Memorial Wesleyan Methodist Church, was "home" to staff and children of Hephzibah for many years. In the 1950s it was difficult to get a pastor for the church. The Georgia District minutes record that four years the church was left "in the hands of the conference president." In 1955, a lady, Rev. Louise Kerr, was pastor.

Tyler Memorial Wesleyan Church in Macon (Morgan Street)

Church service (1985)

Then Rev. W. H. Hampton took the church and continued until 1967. His contribution to the spiritual lives of children and staff was immeasurable.

His service was followed by Rev. Robert Moore, who served from 1967-1970. The next pastor was Rev. M. L. Arnold, who had served as interim superintendent of Hephzibah in 1969 just before the Neymans came.

The last pastor to serve for any length of time was Rev. Paul Busch, whose tenure began in 1973 and continued until 1977.

At times the church's constituency seemed to be largely Hephzibah staff and children. The problem is evident in this note from a January 1975 newsletter from Hephzibah during Mr. Weaver's superintendency:

"These young people need a growing, thriving, enthusiastic church to attend, where they will see other young people besides themselves and where they will see Wesleyan Methodism at work and doing something. The workers at the Home are not in a position to assume the full load of the church, but there are only a few other laymen. We're praying that families will move in, or come in from the community."

The staff children were involved as much as possible. The older teens were often Wesleyan Youth president or other officers. Staff members served in the Wesleyan Missionary Society and in other ways.

Shirley Neyman was president of the WMS at one time and recalls her efforts to get people to give self-denial offerings. One of the junior girls at the Home prayed for God to show her what she should give. Later she came to her houseparent crying.

"What has happened?" she was asked.

"God wants me to give the money I've been saving to buy Christmas gifts! And here it is. I have $5.37! Part of me doesn't want to give it. But I know I'll be helping someone in another land and that makes me happy!"

Her sacrifice inspired other children to give to missions.

In 1983 it seemed best for the Home to go back to the plan of having its own services. Hephzibah Chapel held its meetings in the gym, and Rev. Mike Manley was pastor. From 1984 to 1985, Joe Neyman pastored the chapel.

Then in 1985 Joe's son, Fred, became pastor. He shared his parents' concern for the young people at Hephzibah and through the years had traveled to churches and conferences presenting the Home. Handsome and energetic, Fred was cut out to be a youth pastor. Knowing it would take much care and prayer to salvage the Hephzibah children, he declared, "Kids need a good role model. Jesus taught His disciples by living it before them. My goal with these teens is to give them as much one-on-one discipling as possible."

In summer the Hephzibah children go to church camp and some of the teens through the years have attended area and denominational youth conventions.

Fred Neyman resigned from the pastoral duties in 1991 and the district appointed Joe Neyman to carry that added responsibility. In 1993 Gary Wyatt was named by the Georgia District Board of Administration to serve in this capacity. Members of the Board of Directors once again found themselves wrestling with questions regarding the viability of the campus worship plan.

Chapter 15

The Nineties—
An Era of Change

As early as 1982 the Board of Directors had begun to grapple with an awareness that the 15-acre campus could not accommodate the growing needs of Hephzibah Children's Home. In 1984 the board took a step of faith, purchasing 186 acres of choice land lying along Zebulon Road and Interstate 475. Trusting in God's timing and provisions, the board agreed to avoid indebtedness as they followed God's unfolding plan for an expanded Hephzibah Children's Home. During the 80s the board focused on paying for the new land and developing a master plan. Change was anticipated, but no one could have envisioned how rapidly and how extensively change would occur in the 90s.

In June 1992, a young man who had formerly lived at Hephzibah Children's Home filed charges against Joe Neyman alleging a personal impropriety. Joe denied the charges. The court dismissed the charges. The Hephzibah Children's Home Board of Directors found no evidence for the charges. Nonetheless, Joe immediately resigned as General Director, insisting it was in the best interest of Hephzibah Children's Home. In April 1993, the Board of Directors voted the following resolution of affirmation:

> *Whereas, Rev. T. Joe Neyman has devoted 22½ years in administrative leadership to HCH [Hephzibah Children's*

Home], during which time notable progress has been made in the numbers of persons served and the quality of services provided;

Whereas, Rev. T. Joe Neyman resigned from the position of General Director of Hephzibah Children's Home in June 1992, under the extenuating circumstances of abuse charges for which Hephzibah Children's Home has found no basis; and

Whereas, Upon the dropping of said charges Rev. T. Joe Neyman did in fact reapply and was receiving consideration with the other applicants for the position of General Director of Hephzibah Children's Home when he subsequently requested that his application be withdrawn;

Resolved, That gratitude be expressed to Rev. T. Joe Neyman for his devoted service to Hephzibah Children's Home spanning 22½ years of leadership; and

Resolved, That the Hephzibah Children's Home Board of Directors herewith warmly affirms Rev. T. Joe Neyman as a person of integrity, moral uprightness and devotion to God and the Church.

The Board of Directors was now unexpectedly confronted with the need to advertise for and select a new General Director. From a field of excellent candidates, on January 30, 1993, the board chose Dr. Larry E. Freels of Lexington, Kentucky.

A New Man at the Helm

Larry was born May 19, 1941, the third of Glenn and Nellie Freels' five children. Mr. Freels, a non-believer, was a coal miner in eastern Tennessee. Seeking an improved life for his family he moved them to Frankfort, Indiana, in 1947. Soon after their relocation they were contacted by members of the Michigantown Pilgrim Holiness Church. Through the love and prayers of this congregation, Mr. and Mrs. Freels were converted. From that time

Barbara and Larry Freels

forward, God, the church and raising a Christian family became their focus.

In spite of this influence, it was not until Larry reached age 20, in the summer of 1961, that he surrendered to God and experienced the radical change of God's saving grace in his life.

Soon after his conversion, he began to date Barbara, the 16th child born to Harry and Gladys Slack of Delphi, Indiana (who can say how much Barbara's siblings contributed to her preparation for future service at Hephzibah Children's Home?). Larry and Barbara were married September 14, 1963. About a year after their marriage, Larry accepted God's call to full-time Christian ministry. He immediately enrolled in Frankfort Pilgrim Bible College, where in 1967 he received his Bachelor of Arts degree. During this time Barbara worked and they had their first child, Larry Allen.

In 1967 Larry and Barbara moved to Wilmore, Kentucky, where Larry received his Master of Divinity degree from Asbury Theological Seminary in 1970 and his Doctor of Ministry in 1981. For the next 12 years they pastored the people at Highland Avenue Wesleyan Church, Covington, Kentucky. During these years Barbara gave birth to their two youngest children, Teresa and Eric.

In 1982 the Freels moved to Lexington, Kentucky, and assumed pastoral leadership of the Stonewall Wesleyan Church and served at Asbury Theological Seminary as the Director of the Wesleyan Seminary Foundation. Larry served in this dual role for four years and continued an additional seven years as Senior Pastor at Stonewall Wesleyan Church.

When called to Hephzibah, Larry and Barbara wasted no time in collecting the reins of leadership, winning the hearts of the people and placing their mark on the ongoing ministry of the Home.

The Mission Revisited

The purpose for Hephzibah Children's Home has always been to provide love for the unloved, care for the neglected and Christ's promise of hope for the hopeless. In earlier years the children who came to Hephzibah seemed to be lower risk. But the decade of the 90s ushered in growing numbers of high-risk children with greater needs.

Dr. Freels and his staff quickly discovered they could not enjoy the luxury of asking ". . . are we safe if we take this child into our Home?" Rather, anytime a space opened at Hephzibah, they were challenged by the question, ". . . which child has the

Dominic, Fabian and Shameika were Dr. Freels's first admissions

greatest needs and how can we help that child?" Obviously, this kind of fine-tuning of the Home's philosophical approach was felt across the campus. With change came an initial skyrocketing of behavioral problems and multiplying of psychological needs. The staff cried for help. A dual response plan was initiated.

First, more training for the staff became essential. The entry-level qualifications were increased significantly. Second, a consistent network of professional people qualified to address the psychological and behavioral needs of the children was developed. In God's providence, a local Christian psychiatrist, psychologist and family therapist agreed to assist in evaluating and addressing the needs of the children. These changes resulted in a heightened staff comfort level and a welcomed rise in morale.

The Three Rs Don't Always Come Easy

Reference has already been made to the "on again, off again" relationship Hephzibah Children's Home has had with the Macon Public Schools. Historically the Hephzibah educational pursuit had always followed an "either/or" concept. Except for the few children who worked independently on the General Equivalency Degree (GED) study plan, all the children were either taught on campus or in the public schools. Returning the educational emphasis to a campus school worked well in the 80s. Increased numbers of the students graduated from both high school and college.

As other changes transpired, Dr. Freels and the staff became convinced the "single plan" concept was no longer providing the quality education to which Hephzibah was committed. The learning gap between high achievers and slow learners was growing. A better way than any previously attempted was urgently needed.

Once again the campus school was discontinued. An annual assessment process was administered for each child. Based on the achievement levels and unique needs revealed by the assessment process, the child was then placed in one of six educational opportunities. These included the services of special education, public schools, private Christian schools and the GED program. As needed, private tutoring was also provided on campus. It goes without saying that each of these options carries daily challenges. However, the change to an individualized, custom-tailored approach to meet each child's educational needs holds great promise.

"It's Time for Church"

By 1990 the Board of Directors was again grappling with questions regarding the viability of the campus worship plan. The Macon Wesleyan

Church had been closed and the property sold. The campus ministry had seemed the only valid worship option. However, the total responsibility for speaking, teaching, musical leadership and discipling fell not on a pastor and church staff, but on the Hephzibah Children's Home staff. These were the same people who supervised meal times, administered discipline, conducted daily devotions, helped with homework and set bedtimes. This arrangement was contributing to staff burnout. To whom could they turn for spiritual nurturing? When they yearned for a pastoral prayer, to whom could they look?

A high percentage of the children arrived at Hephzibah having had no prior worship experience. Hephzibah's on-campus church experience seldom involved any persons other than those who would sit down together at the dinner table an hour later.

These concerns for the spiritual nurturing of both staff and children brought Dr. Freels and the board to the conviction, that a less provincial arrangement must be developed. Therefore, beginning in September 1994, the board reluctantly, but with conviction, permitted each set of houseparents to choose from a short list of approved churches in Macon the congregation of which they and their children would become a part. Though not Wesleyan, all approved churches were evangelical congregations teaching the Wesleyan-Arminian doctrine of salvation and sanctification. The houseparents and children were expected to be involved in the full range of services provided by that congregation. The benefits from this change in worship philosophy proved notable. The children could now learn how a local body of believers worship and interact with each other. Children and staff alike would be challenged by pastors, Sunday school teachers, youth leaders, and others in the body of faith.

In 1997, the Georgia District launched the planting of a new congregation in Macon, Georgia. Rev. and Mrs. Mark Atkinson accepted the call to serve as church planters. It was mutually agreed to not disrupt the existing worship schedule of house-parents and children. As quickly as the new church is viable and ready to nurture the children and their houseparents, their worship may once again be unitedly served by The Wesleyan Church.

Moving to "The Promised Land"

The 1984 decision to purchase the 186-acre parcel of land on Zebulon Road had seemed like a giant step of faith. In retrospect, it appeared more like a child's unsteady toddle when compared with the actual demands of relocation.

The logistical challenge was awesome. Funding of the new campus construction was, to a significant degree, dependent on sale of the small Forsyth Road campus. For the greater part of a century Forsyth Road had been home to Hephzibah Children's Home. Now, commercial and professional developments surrounding this site had enhanced its market value. Hephzibah would need to sell this property to make possible the development of the new land. Hephzibah could not sell and surrender occupancy, however, until the new campus was ready to occupy. It was like the proverbial "vicious circle."

Potential buyers came and went—eager to acquire the old campus property, but understandably unwilling to advance payment while permitting the children's home to continue using the campus during the months of construction. Site development, creation of the needed infrastructure (including three-fourths of a mile of finished roadway) and construction of a 6,500 sq. ft. administration building, an 11,000 sq. ft. dinning hall and four 8,000 sq. ft. care residences appeared to be a daunting assignment. Yet that was the minimum development which could allow relocation and continued operation of the Hephzibah Children's Home ministries.

Encouraged by Dr. Freels' leadership, the board concluded in April 1994 that they had agonized over the decision long enough. Even though the Forsyth Road campus had not yet sold, the time had come to begin the march to the "promised land." It was decided that at least the water and utilities must be brought to the site and the road must be constructed (volunteers had cleared the brush and cut the trees the previous year). The three-year capital campaign organized in the summer of 1993, along with beginning returns from the work of Opal Cessna, a consultant hired in mid-1993, provided sufficient monies to assure a beginning.

Architectural drawings had been filed with the appropriate civic offices and before the end of 1993, all needed city and county permits had been issued. Momentum was building. Still, the Forsyth Road property had not sold and the board's commitment to build by faith— without incurring indebtedness—was reaffirmed as a controlling pledge. It had become clear by this time that the earlier intent to hire a contractor was not feasible. Beginning in the fall of 1993, the concept of volunteer mission work teams was first promoted. By the spring of 1994, it was evident that a response of unprecedented proportions was occurring.

The General Board of Administration of The Wesleyan Church had authorized Hephzibah Children's Home Board of Directors to issue an appeal to the Wesleyan churches throughout North America for a three-year annual offering. In faith that the 1994 offering would be sufficient to underwrite costs for site development, the Board of Directors gave the go-ahead. God honored that step of faith. That single offering exceeded $250,000. So, with these early steps—both fearful and courageous—the relocation of Hephzibah Children's Home was launched.

Yes, one of the most dramatic changes experienced in the 90s was the move to a new home . . . a new campus! Hephzibah Children's Home had traveled a long distance from that January day in 1900 and from the old farm house in Bolingbroke, Georgia. Bettie and Mollie Tyler may have experienced loneliness during their move to Bolingbroke in 1900. In contrast, Dr. Freels and his staff had nearly 2,000 volunteer Wesleyans who came to walk and work at their side to make the 1994-1997 relocation a reality. But this was just one miracle of many more to come.

Chapter 16

But the Lord ...

* Narrated by Dr. Larry E. Freels to Dr. Ronald R. Brannon.

Believers are people of faith. Why, then, are we taken by surprise when God chooses to intervene in our lives and surrounding circumstances? Yet, I confess to shock and amazement more than a few times during those years of the Hephzibah Children's Home relocation. There were repeated interventions in events and circumstances that can only be attributed to God. There may be some who would ascribe those happenings to mere chance or luck. Those months heightened my belief in God's sovereignty and the conviction that He is prepared to control the smallest events of life. He can reverse man's decisions, turn the direction of man's thoughts and regulate the time-table of happenings with inexplicable precision.

My personal chapter in this chronicle began in the fall of 1993. I stood on the edge of the timbered 180-acre land to which Hephzibah Children's Home purposed to relocate. The site was perfect. The plans were exciting. The cost was awesome. My personal sense of inadequacy was overwhelming. The assignment to lead in this massive project was frightening. I knew God had called me to this ministry and surely He would see me through. Yet, humanly, there was the temptation to recoil. "The task is too big for me." But the Lord ...

I have been reminded of Peter stepping out of the boat on the water. The miracle didn't start while he was in the boat. It seemed I was in a boat with Peter. I stepped out of the boat . . . and the miracle began to happen. Almost immediately, God began a process of bringing the right person, at the exact time of need, with the precise skills to resolve a specific problem. Let me tell you about it.

Massive amounts of site preparation needed to be done before construction could commence. My college and seminary training for ministry had not equipped me for supervision of such a major construction project. I couldn't do that. But the Lord . . .

I don't remember his name. He was returning to Michigan from a vacation in the South. He seemed to be just one of many we welcome to the campus. However, upon his return home that summer day in 1994, he became God's messenger. Within two weeks, a call came from Bob Rogers of Prolime Services in Washington, Michigan. Our campus visitor was a friend of his. He had told Bob about Hephzibah's relocation project, as well as our ministry to at-risk kids. In response to Mr. Rogers' call, and at his request, I sent a packet of information. A short time later he called again. This second call was to coordinate a visit to the campus. He and his family paid that visit on Labor Day weekend, 1994. Little did either of us know what a key role Bob would play in development of God's plan.

My fears and feelings of inadequacy concerning leadership of the project had been real. But the Lord . . .

Bob Rogers became God's miracle agent for initial leadership of the volunteer forces. In addition to his construction skills and experience, he brought his own heavy earth moving equipment and agreed to spend the entire winter on site. Further, he brought an infectious enthusiasm which helped inspire other skilled people to become involved in the project. Soon there was identified a roster of skilled, heavy equipment operators from across the Church— persons willing to come to Macon for a limited time for work. In addition to the skilled mechanics, there were hundreds of semi-skilled volunteers. They came from as far as Wyoming in the west, New York in the east, Florida in the south and Canada in the north. Almost every week from October 1994 through 1998, there were skilled

Bob Rogers, volunteer from Washington, Michigan

operators, supported by hard working volunteers. How else could Hephzibah clear the brush and timber, build nearly a mile of road, excavate (or fill) sites for the six initial buildings, install water lines, prepare the way for the utility company to bury electrical cables, and construct six beautiful buildings?

Bob Pierce, volunteer from North Carolina

"It just can't be accomplished with volunteers." But the Lord . . .

Time after time, the work was interrupted by forbidding circumstances. Humanly it appeared certain we faced damaging delays. There was the week we urgently needed a surveyor to confirm elevations for the building sites. Local companies were committed to other projects—and besides, they were expensive. At that precise time, God sent a visitor. A Christian from another denomination, he happened to stop. Never before had he visited the Hephzibah campus. He knew no one on the staff. He simply had heard about Hephzibah Children's Home. He was enroute to Haiti to perform a volunteer service to a mission there, but had three extra days in his travel schedule. He was a civil engineer and had his equipment in the van. As he turned to leave, he quietly said, "No charge, just a blessing to be a little help." The work "should have" suffered delay. But the Lord

Then there was the rock problem. Bob Rogers reported that one area of the road and construction site was not getting done because of a massive outcropping of rock. Even his huge bulldozers couldn't move it. Did we know anyone who was familiar with stone blasting? We didn't. That very week, a call came from Bob Pierce of MAPCO, INC. in North Carolina. Mr. Pierce had worshipped in a Wesleyan church the prior Sunday evening and had seen a brochure telling of the Hephzibah relocation project. He reported that his company did road building for the state and wondered if we could use those kind of skills—which included rock blasting and removal. Within a few days he was on site and the "impossible" problem of stone out-cropping was resolved. Even Bob Rogers's bulldozer couldn't move it. But the Lord . . .

Great progress was being made, but we needed a road grader for the final "pre-paving" touches on the road. We had gone as far as possible without that piece of equipment. Through World Gospel Mission we had heard of a contractor named Bob Peed in Butler, Georgia. Though a stranger to us, we called to inquire if he could help us locate the needed

Nancy Self, volunteer from Cherryville, NC

equipment. His immediate answer was, "Yes, I have one sitting idle right now." Where was it? "In Macon, Georgia!" "I'll be glad to loan it to you. Call Mr. Cook and on my authorization, ask him to bring it over to you." Mr. Cook was already hauling the gravel to the new campus. Within hours he had delivered the grader. When asked about the cost of rental, Bobby Peed said in his southern style, "I'm just glad to be able to help you all out. There will be no charge." We had reached the place where the road building process appeared halted. But the Lord . . .

Volunteers were ready to install the water main. It was required, though, that a Georgia licensed plumber apply for the permit and oversee the work. Through Mr. Peed we were put in contact with Pyle Plumbing, Inc. Mr. Pyle agreed to obtain the permit and examine and approve the work of our volunteers. He also volunteered to order the materials through his company for our payment without mark-up, thus saving Hephzibah nearly $10,000.

Two volunteer work teams were scheduled to arrive the week we planned to install the water main. Bob Pierce, who was returning with a team from North Carolina, could oversee the installation while the other volunteers would help. Unknown to us, the leader of the other work team from Evansville, Indiana, was a 25-year employee of the Evansville Water Company, with a wealth of experience installing water mains. Had we known, we would have planned it that way. But the Lord . . .

The time came to make decisions concerning the lighting of the roadway. In negotiating with Georgia Power we learned their package mandated both installation and maintenance of the system—at an ongoing charge of $400 per month. The day before we were to meet with Georgia Power to finalize a plan, I received a call from Dave Barber in Gillette, Wyoming. He had sensed God's tug on his heart to volunteer help with the relocation project. He wondered how he might use his state electrician's license and his skills in installing major electric lines and lights. He agreed to come and oversee the installation of our outdoor light system. It had begun to look like there was only one option. But the Lord . . .

By the winter of 1995 it had become evident that the tremendous response and availability of volunteer mission work teams called for the naming of a full time construction supervisor. The problem, though, was compound. Hephzibah Children's Home had no money to hire such a person. Further, there was no qualified person in sight even if monies suddenly became available. Once again the mountain of impossibility loomed tall. But the Lord . . .

In the spring of 1995 Bob Rogers called and said, "Larry, I have your man." I responded, "What do you mean? We don't have any money to move a man here or to pay his salary." Bob responded, "Larry, don't worry about the money. Bring him down for an interview and we'll go from there."

Tom Wirsing,
construction supervisor

So it was that Tom and Joyce Wirsing became key players in the Hephzibah story, arriving in July 1995. With the encouragement of Bob Rogers and the leadership of District Superintendent Kenneth Boschee, the East Michigan District assumed most of the Wirsings' salary obligation for the first year. Tom proved to be the ideal man for that strategic job. He knew construction, he knew people, and he had a servant's heart. Joyce also brought needed strengths to the growing ministries of Hephzibah Children's Home, stepping into the dietician's assignment where she served with distinction for two years. The Wirsings initially came "for at least one year." However, by year's end, the Hephzibah miracle had so captured their hearts and they had become so indispensable that they committed to the expansion project on a long-term basis.

One Monday morning the local Wal-Mart warehouse called with the information they had several skids of materials which they would give Hephzibah Children's Home. There was a catch however. It was necessary that these items be picked up by 1:00 p.m. that day. They further advised that there would be need for a flatbed truck equipped with a tow motor. Of course, Hephzibah Children's Home doesn't have a flatbed truck . . . and Wal-Mart had offered a very small window of time. Emotionally, I knew it was impossible! But the Lord . . .

I looked out the window and there in the parking lot was a large flatbed truck equipped with a tow motor. A work team from North Carolina had just arrived for a week of missionary work service. It just

Volunteers came in all sizes

happened that one member of the team had agreed with his company to deliver some equipment enroute to Macon. Hence the truck. To his surprise he was soon on his way to Wal-Mart. Was that mere luck? I think not.

In addition to these rather dramatic ways in which God intervened in the early stages of this project, there were hundreds of daily providences which were no less significant. We rejoiced over good construction weather, safety for the hundreds of volunteers, courtesies from local businesses to assist and save costs and a $21,000 gift from the Bibb County Exchange Club for a new in-ground swimming pool on the new campus.

By January 1996 the road was constructed and the ground was ready to construct the six initial buildings. The call was issued to those who had volunteered their services. It was breathtaking to see the response. They came by the hundreds. There were the skilled, semi-skilled and unskilled. They gave their time, pouring out their energies in joyous gifts of love to the hundreds of at-risk children who in future years shall find hope and help at Hephzibah Children's Home. By the spring of 1996 all six buildings were under roof and secure from the weather.

Still the workmen arrived. They came from Canada and virtually every district in the USA. Miracles became a daily expectation. There were skilled laborers who arrived in their own RVs and stayed the entire winter. Others stayed only a few days. They completed plumbing and electrical installations. They did finish work and painted. A professional painter from Michigan was on campus for an extended time to supervise the interior painting. A professional paperhanger came to oversee the wallpaper project. A local linen store owner provided the window dressings at cost and closed her store for one day in order to free her employees to come and install the drapes and blinds. A professional carpet layer from North Carolina spent weeks laying over 7,000 sq. yards of carpet. A local foundation gave enough money to purchase most of the office furniture. Much of the care residences' furniture and supplies was

Volunteers raise wall for new Home

138

made available at a greatly reduced cost from a friend in High Point, North Carolina. He made numerous trips to Hephzibah and gave generously of his time. All of the appliances were made available at wholesale cost from an appliance store owner in Georgia. Electrical supplies and equipment were purchased from a local provider at greatly reduced prices. Ed Harrington, from the Central Holland church in Michigan, stayed for the entire time. He primarily supervised the construction of the dining hall. Bob Pierce from North Carolina brought his equipment and employees to lay the asphalt for the road and parking lots. Hephzibah's only cost

Ed Harrington, volunteer working on new entrance sign

was for the material. A local interior decorator donated time and expertise.

By the early summer of 1996, with all six buildings under roof but none ready to use, the building fund was depleted. Those in charge estimated it would require about $1.5 million to complete the relocation phase. On one hand, such an amount seemed a staggering sum. On the other hand, however, the board had been led to believe that the Forsyth Road campus, when sold, would net at least that sum. Based on those assurances the Board of Directors now felt for the first time that a construction loan would be acceptable. The work could thus be continued without interruption and the obligation paid in full upon the sale of the former campus. Accordingly, Hephzibah Children's Home borrowed from the Wesleyan Investment Foundation the sum of $1.4 million for completion of the relocation phase.

Dr. Larry Freels, General Director, assisted by (l. to r.): Shamieka Kimball, James Maxwell, Mario Chambers & Chris Bryant, who spoke for the children.

Because the people had a mind to work (Nehemiah 4:6) the first phase of the campus construction was finished. The formal dedication took place April 12, 1997. Hundreds of friends, church, state and local dignitaries arrived to participate in the glorious "once in a lifetime" event. Prevailing throughout

Hephzibah children on Dedication Day,
April 12, 1997

Dr. Virgil Mitchell leading
prayer with Dr. Larry Freels
at the ground breaking

the day's celebratory atmosphere was one overriding conviction. The day would never have arrived but for the Lord!

Due to a few unfinished final touches required by the strict standards of State regulations for childcare, the actual relocation was delayed another ten weeks. Finally on July 1, 1997, the physical relocation of Hephzibah Children's Home to the new Zebulon Road campus was triumphantly finalized.

There were those who had declared, "you can't accomplish such a major project relying almost solely on volunteers. Interest will wane. Even a well funded construction company would have required at least a year of continuous labor to develop such a campus." But the Lord...

Over 2,000 volunteer workers have invested themselves in this mission. Each has come at personal cost for travel and on-site housing and Hephzibah has provided meals. A professional audit company in Macon, Georgia, estimated that the volunteers have saved the Home between $1.5 million and $2 million, thus enabling Hephzibah to achieve this goal. This dream has been realized not by huge grants, but from hundreds of churches, families and friends giving what they could.

Now timing of the sale of the Forsyth Road campus became urgent. A construction loan of $1.4 million awaited payoff. While it waited, interest mounted. Seemingly good contracts would approach deadline dates and then dissipate. There was the confidence that God who had so miraculously brought Hephzibah Children's Home to this place would not abandon the ministry now. Construction of the Elizabeth Home for unwed mothers was put on hold. In an effort to enhance sale possibilities the property was re-platted into five units.

This change led to the sale of a back one-fourth of the old campus in the spring of 1998. That transaction made it possible to reduce the construction loan $200,000 and freed $80,000 to do grading on the

Forsyth Road campus. This grading was urgently needed to make the land more marketable.

The board repeatedly approved other contracts for purchase—but just before they sold—they didn't.

It was decided that the vacant buildings—and the incumbent costs for razing them—might be a deterrent to prospective buyers. The board authorized receiving bids to raze the old buildings. Those bids called for an expense of $200,000 to remove the buildings and properly dispose of the refuse. These were immediately rejected. But the Lord . . . and His people . . .

Once again volunteers were told of the need. Equipment was borrowed or rented. In just over one week approximately 100 volunteers completed the task. Trusses and other expensive timbers

New entry sign

New junior boys cottage

were salvaged from the old buildings. The cement blocks and bricks were crushed and hauled to the Zebulon Road property and stock-piled there to be used as base for roads that will be constructed in future phases. Rather than costing $200,000, the cost was held to less than $50,000.

At that juncture, with the buildings and trees removed and grading in process, the Forsyth Road campus became dramatically attractive to developers. The broker began to receive numerous inquiries. The log-jam broke. It had begun to look impossible, But the Lord . . .

By early August 1998, the Forsyth Road campus was sold. The construction debt was paid in total. The $5.7 million relocation was accomplished without indebtedness. Construction of the Elizabeth Home was returned to active status. The future again appeared as bright as God's promises.

Hephzibah Children's Home began nearly 100 years ago. Someone said at that time, "It's a wild undertaking. . . . You'll all freeze or starve." They didn't. Some may have been tempted to echo the same sentiment upon hearing of plans to relocate, to increase facilities to care for not just 40 children but 120 children and to open the Elizabeth Home Ministries for young, unwed mothers-to-be.

Our reply to those who ask "How can these things be?" is simply:

But the Lord *was my support. He also brought me out into a broad place; He delivered me because He delighted in me.* Psalm 18:18b-19

But you shall be called Hephzibah . . . For the Lord delights in you. Isaiah 62:4

Dr. Freels celebrates sale of the Forsyth property

142

Chapter 17

Shirley Finds a Home

What ever became of the little Shirley with whom this chronicle began?

God's eye was on His little sparrow in a foster home in High Point, North Carolina. He had blessed Shirley Ann Locklear with a church family at Hayworth Wesleyan Church where they lovingly put up with her independent ways.

One Sunday Pauline and Sally Edmonds invited her for lunch after service. While at their house she picked up Pauline's Bible. A little pamphlet fell out that had on it a picture of a man and a woman.

"Who are these people?" Shirley asked.

"Oh, that's Joe and Shirley Neyman. They run our children's home in Georgia. I wish you could go there. It would be a wonderful place for you!"

By the time they finished describing it, Shirley was convinced. When no one was looking, she took the little pamphlet and tucked it away. Later she learned that the Hayworth pastor, Rev. Dawalt, and a caseworker were making arrangements for her to go to Hephzibah. One night, lying on the top bunk at the Brown's house, she wrote a letter by the light of a street lamp shining through the window. Below is the unedited letter, dated June 1, 1971.

Dear Sherly and Joe,

I am a 13-year-old girl. My name is Shirland Locklear. I attend Hayworth Memorial Church. The pastor is Rev. Dawalt. If you know any of my friends, they are all helping me.

Please accept me, please I am begging from my heart. I had family problems, and my friends helped me, and I am in a foster home. They said that after school was out I would be going to where you are. I hope so. I have got Missionary Nursing on my mind, that's what I'm working for, but the way I'm going now I will never make it. I a nice Christian girl, who loves to tend to children, clean up, I use to help lots of people clean up. You can call to High Point and ask anyone who attends Hayworth. Mrs. Sherly and Mr. Joe, my hold life is going away. My friends have helped me so much, they all said being with you and others would help me too. I'm easy to get along with.

Please take me, please, they said I would be going to where you are after school is out, what if I don't get to, there goes my life's future. You know! God is giving me the strength to write this letter. What would we do without him? Please take me. If you don't, what will I do? Write back or call or do something. So I will feel much better, I haven't been feeling very good about anything recently. Help me solve my worries.

I must close. May God help you.

Shirland Locklear

Later Joe Neyman came and visited Shirley in the foster home. She kept hoping she could soon leave the Browns'.

Then her foster parents went away for a weekend and left Shirley with the three boys. She knew minors should not be left in the care of another minor. This was her chance, she decided. Calling Pauline and Sally, she told them the situation. They came for a visit and then reported it to the authorities.

It was not long before she was moved to a foster home in Gibsonville with an older couple whose children were grown and married. One other foster child was there, a little girl. But to Shirley's delight she had a carpeted bedroom all her own. These foster parents were wonderful. Shirley felt like her problems were over. She forgot about the letter she had written. She forgot about Mr. Neyman's visit. She was happy at last!

But arrangements had already been made for her to go to Hephzibah. So she was uprooted once more, and one day a car came driving up to take her away. In the car were Joe and Shirley Neyman and their children, Fred and Darlynda.

Once again Shirley felt fear and insecurity, and the adjustment to life at the Home was not easy. She walked into the senior girls' cottage and met the stares of a group of strange girls. Housemother Dorothy Allison tried to ease her fears with her kind greeting and showed her to her room. Was she trying to express her frustrations when that night she laid her pillow on the floor between the two beds and cried herself to sleep? Her roommate was at college and home only on the weekends.

The very next day Mrs. Neyman took her to the health department for a check-up and to get shots. Shirley was terrified, but Mrs. Neyman, with a stern look, said, "You'd better straighten up. You're too big to act like that!" After that experience, Shirley told Mrs. Neyman her name was "Miss Cruel" and that became a joke!

Gradually Shirley got into the routine. In the mornings the children waited in the dining hall to catch the school bus. Sometimes she went early to vacuum the carpet in Mr. Neyman's office. One day she saw the superintendent on his knees and heard him praying for food to be supplied. Later that week Shirley missed school for a dental appointment. After the other children had gone, she went to where the staff met for their prayer meeting. And there she got to witness the answer to Mr. Neyman's prayer. A big truck pulled up the driveway to the dining hall. The freezers of the Piggly Wiggly store down the road had quit working and they had to get rid of all their frozen food. The staff and children enjoyed shrimp, pizzas, and many other delicacies. Another time the Pet Milk Company truck had a accident and brought the ice cream to the Home.

Prayer and miracles just went together, Shirley found. She knew her housemother, Mrs. Allison, prayed in her bathroom every morning, for she had heard her different times when she knocked at her door to ask a question.

David and Shirley (1980)

145

Shirley found that Mrs. Allison knew how to make her girls feel special. Once a month she took a girl out to eat. She planned a party for each birthday. Delicious snacks were provided for their "family" time each evening. And Mrs. Allison was faithful in having devotions with her girls. Dorothy would explain how they could apply it to their lives.

The Neymans were special people to Shirley. Mr. Neyman would get the children to work for him and then would pay them. He was the first man Shirley ever trusted. He spent time with them, playing ball, teasing them, but disciplining if that was required. Mrs. Neyman made sure the children had what they needed, took them shopping, and cared for their medical needs. Fred and Darlynda were like a brother and sister to Shirley.

Her favorite person at Hephzibah was Geraldine Fortune. A patient, loving person, Geraldine put up with Shirley's awkwardness and stubbornness and never scolded her harshly. This amazed Shirley after the rough treatment she had endured with her parents. Once she spilled the paint when Geraldine was painting her hallway. Another time Shirley knocked over the stand which held all the plants Geraldine had spent the morning repotting. Each time Shirley was afraid Geraldine wouldn't love her anymore. But Geraldine always gave her a hug and the assurance of her continued love.

The long summer holiday with camping, trips to swim and boat at Lake Tobasofkee, picnics and a trip to Six Flags every year; the exciting holiday times with sumptuous meals; the Christmases with all the wonderful gifts—these helped make Hephzibah a place Shirley loved.

She helped make one Hephzibah board meeting a memorable one. Some of the board members brought their wives. Among them was Lois, first wife of Dr. C. Wesley Lovin. Shirley discovered Lois could not ride a bicycle and proposed to correct this on the spot. Mrs. Lovin was willing and while the board deliberated, Shirley kept holding up the bicycle and pushing while her pupil tried to learn her balance.

After supper when everyone was outside, Shirley said to Mrs. Lovin, "Do you think you're ready to ride by yourself?"

"I'll try," she replied.

So Shirley announced, "Mrs. Lovin's going to ride a bicycle!"

She got on and Shirley pushed her around the corner of the office and then said, "I'm going to let you go!"

"I'm not sure if I can do it!" Lois cried.

But it was too late! Legs stuck out, bike wobbling, she careened off the drive, across the lawn and into the pecan orchard, yelling, "Somebody help me stop this bicycle! Stop this bicycle!"

Suddenly she stopped, falling over in a heap, unhurt, and joining in the laughter echoing down from the watching crowd.

Today Shirley treasures many memories of the place that gave her love and security. Churches across the denomination helped make this possible. On her sixteenth birthday she received a dozen pink roses from the Kirkville, New York, Wesleyan Church. They also made her a lovely birthday quilt. Another treasure is a beautiful clown quilt made by the Shady Grove Church in Colfax, North Carolina.

Shirley graduated from Central Wesleyan College in 1980 and that fall married David Duncan. Today, they both serve on the Hephzibah Children's Home staff in church relations.

Many other diamonds in the rough, unlovely because of life's adversities, have been polished and made useful by their experiences at Hephzibah.

fine
(fë`nå)

The final chord of a musical composition is often designated by the word "fine" which is pronounced "(fë`nå)." It marks the conclusion. There is the more common pronunciation of the word "fine" which means "excellent, very good."

This chapter is not "fë`nå," the conclusion of the Hephzibah story. It is "fine—excellent, very good" for the work shall go on. It shall go on because the new campus is equipped to serve for countless years. It shall go on because a dedicated staff is committed to keep "stepping in" to champion the cause of needy and neglected children. It shall go on because people across the continent translate their love for at-risk children into the support needed to fund this ministry. It shall go on because it is the "delight" of God.

It shall go on as long as those whom the home has served keep coming back to lift a load and to confirm that it pays. That is really "fine!"

Take Russell Luther. He came to Hephzibah Children's Home at age ten. He was a typical lad hungering for a loving environment and someone in whom he could place trust. He remained at Hephzibah ten years. After graduating from high school he enrolled in Southern Wesleyan University (SWU). Thanks to an SWU Co-op program with Clemson University, he graduated with a math/computer science major and a business administration minor. Upon completion of his college program, he returned to Macon, Georgia, where he secured an excellent job with General Electric Capital Corporation.

During the new campus construction period Russell returned and worked for a month as a volunteer. His company offered select employees a one-month scholarship to work for their favorite charity. He was one of the select. In scheduling his four weeks of service, he explained, "If it weren't for Hephzibah, I wouldn't be here today. Hephzibah saved my life. This is my home. This is the only home I have. This is my family. The friends I made here are still my very best friends. They gave me all the

Russell Luther, former student

opportunities I needed to make it in life. In some small way I want to pay back what Hephzibah has done for me. I love this place and I want to do everything I can to help someone else like myself."

That kind of testimony is better than "fine." Russell made an unforgettable impact on other volunteers, staff and Hephzibah children during those weeks. Yes, the ministry of Hephzibah Children's home shall go on as long as alumni like Russell go out to change their world.

Or consider the story of George Callaway. George is now 75 years of age. Hephzibah became home to him and his brother when he was 12 years old. During the next six and a half years he did his share of chores—building fires in the kitchen stove, cutting and hauling wood, doing laundry, milking cows, farming and gardening. There was also time for school and sports.

As George approached his 19th birthday in 1941, he left Hephzibah to join the military. He had never accepted Christ during his stay at Hephzibah. A short time later, however, at Ft. Bragg, he experienced God's convicting spirit. He testifies that the teachings, prayers and love of Hephzibah's Director Jones and houseparent Mrs. Warren were instrumental in his decision to accept Jesus as his personal Savior. He reports that in the middle of the night in a Ft. Bragg barracks he received the assurance that he "hit the solid rock." He only regrets that he was not a Christian while living at Hephzibah.

George and his wife Helen have spent most of their married lives in New Castle, Indiana. They are blessed by two sons, both successful businessmen, and four grandchildren. From time to time they wend their way southward to revisit Hephzibah. During their most recent stay, while helping with construction, George was heard to say, "I love this place." Isn't that "fine?"

Too many of today's children have yet to discover their personal "lift of love." We can't "touch the tomorrow" of them all, but it's for such as these that Hephzibah Children's Home shall continue to extend her borders. It's the return of alumni like these which provides assurance that it is worth the sacrifice. That kind of encouragement is just "fine." The story shall go on.

This book has been an attempt to project a panoramic view of the works of God over a century of loving service. The heroes and heroines largely remain unknown and unsung. They have been pleased to give the praise to God.

The saga began under the long shadows of the Civil War. With a singleness of purpose, it has brought Hephzibah Children's Home to the 21st Century with cutting edge readiness to provide care for at-risk children. Through the Elizabeth Home, that care shall soon extend to expectant single mothers. Long-range plans not only call for care of at least 130 children, but a full scale recreation center, a pet therapy farm, an outdoor science center, a fishing lake, a daycare for community children and a retirement center for those who want to retire with a mission— the mission of giving a child a second chance by being the hands and love of Jesus Christ.

George Callaway, former student

The final chapter of the Hephzibah story is yet to be written. Leaders and staff are often reminded of the work of One who had no place to call his home. Yet, He reminded that ". . . inasmuch as [we] did it to one of the least of these . . .

[we] did it to [Him]" (Matthew 25:40). When the final chapter is written, it is our prayer that all who served may hear, "Well done (fine, very good!) good and faithful servant; . . . Enter into the joy of your Lord." (Matthew 25:21). (fë`nå)

For more information on impacting the life of a child, please contact:

Hephzibah Children's Home
6601 Zebulon Road
Macon, Georgia 31220-7606
Telephone – 912/477-3383
Fax – 912/474-6370
E-mail – Hephzab101@aol.com.